TESTAMENT

TESTAMENT

TESTAMENT

Belief in an Age of Unbelief
Faith in an Era of Skepticism

STAN PARMISANO, O.P.

AVE MARIA PRESS Notre Dame, Indiana 46556

International Standard Book Number: 0-87793-458-4 (pbk)

0-97793-459-2

Library of Congress Catalog Card Number: 91-72452

Cover and text design by Katherine Robinson Coleman

Printed and bound in the United States of America.

These fragments I have shored against my ruins.

T. S. Eliot

Ordina quest' Amore, O tu que m' ami
(Set this love of mine in order, O you who love me)

Jacopone da Todi

CONTENTS

Foreword ——————————————————————— 9

ONE
I Believe ——————————————————————— 11

TWO
In the Beginning, God ——————————————— 25

THREE
God and World ——————————————————— 49

FOUR
Christianity ———————————————————— 71

FIVE
The Spirit and the Woman ——————————— 93

SIX
Eucharist: Word and Words ————————————— 109

SEVEN
Ministry of the Word ————————————————— 129

EIGHT
Ways of Love —————————————————————— 137

NINE
Intimations of Immortality ——————————— 155

TEN
First and Last Things ———————————————— 167

FOREWORD

Many years ago, toward the end of a retreat I had been directing, a sister challenged me with: "Do you really believe what you've been preaching to us?" I thought she was concerned about my practicing what I preached, so I assured her that I did believe it though I wasn't very good at living up to my belief. To set her more at ease I also told her that my preaching is primarily to myself, to help *me* live my faith as I should. I preached the ideal, trusting that God would, at least eventually, give me added grace to measure up to it.

But as we talked on, it became clear that she wasn't so much interested in the living of faith as in the actual believing. She pretty much knew what we were to believe as Christians, she was aware of the ideal. But did I, and she, actually believe it? This, of course, had long been a concern of mine as well, but I had been more or less content to *believe* that I believed and hope that if I didn't God would bring me to it. "I have faith. Help my lack of faith" (Mk 9:24).

Since that particular retreat the world has turned topsy-turvy and with it, it seems, the church. The objectivity of faith, or of truth in general, is now of little interest compared to its subjectivity. As Thomas More is made to say in Robert Bolt's play: "What matters to me is not whether it's true or not but that I believe it to be true, or rather, not that I *believe* it, but that *I* believe it." Faith is not something apart from us that we are to hold to whatever particular doubts and difficulties we may have with it; it is internal conviction, personal involvement, that matters, whatever adherence to or rejection of a particular creed it may entail.

I'm part of this revolution, at once a producer and product of it. Not, however, as I've learned it from the world; rather

as I've experienced it within the objectivity of my Christian
faith. "Who do people say the Son of Man is?" *Some say
this, some say that.* "But you, . . . who do *you* say I am?" Yes,
I am a personalist, but only because my person is sustained
and developed within something, someone, outside and much
larger than myself: *You are the Christ, the Son of the living
God* (Mt 16:13–16).

Therefore, I find myself continually engaged in matching
my internal belief with what I have received from my Christian heritage. In this process the heritage comes first. Here is
the begetter of my flesh, bone, blood, my first teacher and
lover and challenger toward life, the past and present giver of
the best of gifts. But it is this very heritage that demands that
I question even it, that I think and decide for myself, that I be
honest with myself, that I become whole within myself, with
it, and with the rest of creation. Not all questions are expected
to be answered, not all divisions healed. The questioning as
the growing is to go on till death (and after?). But the movement must always be toward what is beyond myself, which,
yes again, I must judge according as *I* believe, but which I
must also suffer myself to be judged by.

This is something of the dynamic that underlies the bits
and pieces that follow and gives them, I hope, some of the
unity and coherence native to my Christian faith and longed
for by our fragmented world. They are new thoughts and old
about crucial matters of faith, from faith itself to God in the
beginning and God and us now and in the end — reflections,
meditations, sermons preached and to be preached, memories,
images, stories, parables, all returned now to the overall context out of which they were born and in which alone they
have their proper meaning.

ONE

I Believe

Context is everything — or almost. Not the colors and shapes in isolation, but how they touch and blend, excite one another into life, their own and that of the whole — it's this that makes the painting. Not individual words, one at a time, but all together, feeding each other, feeding *on* each other, growing in life and meaning as the sentence, the poem, the story unfolds. The dolphin, happy, sleek, beautiful in deep ocean waters and, having been trapped by the shallows, dying and rotting and stinking, a meal for flies on the dry shore. Sex in the context of a loving marriage and out of it. The old man vacant and alone in a bleak empty room of a cheap hotel on the wrong side of town and as once he was with family and friends in the warmth and cleanness of a home that was his own. The child abandoned and dying in a crowded street in Calcutta (or anywhere) and being loved back to life in the arms of a Mother Teresa. Myself, by myself, cut off from others, only emptiness within and around me, then suddenly God and a whole new world of thought and life and love. Context is almost everything.

Context is background thinking — the meaning that thoughts and words take from it. You're not immediately aware of it, but a sentence or a creed is no longer understood in quite the same way because there's been a shift, minute and subtle, in context, in background. And you've had little if anything to do with it. Society's basic thinking has changed, and so has yours. Consciously you may think as before, your creed still the same, but now it's in a different context, and the context is *within* you. You feel slightly uncomfortable, on edge. There's division within though you can't quite locate it. It's like swimming as the current begins to change. Okay, maybe, if the change were only outside. But it's within you, slowing and gradually wearing you down. Should you just relax and go along with it? You can't, because of your conscious creed recalled in the old context — and because, from what you observe, the current seems to draw to a void, a vortex of night and nothingness. You think you're right, at least your creed still seems the best around, but you're not as sure now as you once were. You've got to struggle to keep afloat. All because of this silent, stealthy shift in background. Context is everything . . .

. . . almost. For the single word or color or person is important too, is part of the context, helping to shape and direct it, for good or for bad. The individual word, color, thought, and life, *my* creed, given and taken, received and pondered and lived — the end product, the final work of art or of life depends on this also. I may not feel quite at home in this shifting world, but the world may have its self-doubts too because of me.

In Peter Schaffer's play *Equus* the child psychologist, depressed over his inability to treat his young patients and dreading the harm he may be doing them, cries out in the end: "I need more desperately than my children need me a way of seeing in the dark." Audiences throughout the world, plagued by many questions but gifted with few if any meaningful answers, immediately recognized the cry as their own. It's a cry, really, for faith.

Because faith, Christian faith at any rate, is this way of "seeing in the dark." It's like a little child behind a dense crowd that's watching a parade. The child hears the music and the cheers and the laughter but can see nothing but the forest of legs that hide the spectacle. So she whimpers and cries and tugs, until finally one looks down, takes the child up and onto his shoulders and so gives her the sight she longs for. So it is with faith. Out of the jumble and jungle of our hearts we cry for help. God hears, stoops down to our level, and raises us to his shoulder so that now we can see what we had only suspected or heard was there.

Or it's like being lost in a dark wood. You want out but you're uncertain of the way. You go in one direction but that doesn't seem right. You head in another but this is unfamiliar too. In the meantime the dark has deepened so that you can scarcely see; and it's become cold, very cold. You begin to panic. You call out. No answer. You call again and keep calling. Nothing. You find yourself shivering, from cold but also from a creeping fear. You sit and huddle against a tree for warmth, and watch the darkness turn to black. Now you really become afraid. Then you notice in the distance flickering pinpoints of light. Illusion? Fireflies? You strain to see. The sparks converge and expand till they become — a flashlight! You call out and next you know there's this shadow of a man standing before you. "What are you doing out here alone? Don't you know you can die of exposure? Come, I'll lead you back to the lodge." And with him as your guide you at last reach safety. Such is the light and guidance of faith.

There are two kinds of knowledge. One is of the brain or head. This is the knowledge of facts and what they add up to. It's the knowledge involved in raw seeing, hearing, feeling, the knowledge we use in making out the budget, scheduling our day, or our lives, in eating a meal or driving a car. It's the knowledge of inference and deduction, of observation and experiment. It's what our Euro-American world most regards

as knowledge and thus as the goal of education — the computer brain with all its intricate, sophisticated hardware and
software.

The other kind is of the heart. It sees beneath and beyond
the facts and reads not so much the lines of a book or paper
or poem as what's between them. It doesn't infer or deduce;
it just knows, instinctively, intuitively, and we don't "know"
how or why. It's a knowledge of underground feeling rather
than above-ground thought, a knowledge that seems to be
given rather than achieved.

It was my mother who first shocked me into the realization
of the magnitude of this second kind of knowledge. I had had
it before, in early childhood and after, when the world, like an
old trunk, would magically open and reveal its ancient hidden
treasures, or when, like St. Paul, I'd momentarily be lifted
into some heaven above the world. But it was Mom who
proved to me the workings of this other layer of mind and
how in this invisible dimension one mind "touches" another.
I was home from college for the weekend and, as usual on
a Saturday night, I was out till two or three in the morning.
I was driving home, quite sober, but, largely because of the
heavy fog, managed to smash into a cab that abruptly stopped
in front of me for a fare. Miraculously, no one was hurt, but
the car was a mess and I had to leave it and walk the rest of
the way home. As I approached my house I saw my mother
sitting at the upstairs' window, her head buried in her hands.
I felt rather than saw her anguish. I ran up the stairs and
into her bedroom. "What is it, what's wrong?" "I just had a
terrible dream," she sobbed. "I dreamt you were dead." Not
quite right, of course, but close enough to make my spine
tingle and my brain wonder. At the moment I almost died she
dreamt that I did. And how much did the dreaming and her
cry within it help keep me alive?

This happened years ago and maybe in the interim the
facts have been clouded over and fiction introduced. But in

my work as a priest I've often seen in others this same kind of knowledge at work even more dramatically and with the facts verifiable. "The heart has reasons that the reason does not know." These are the words of one known the world over for his "head" knowledge; he was in fact one of the world's greatest mathematicians. Blaise Pascal wrote them in light of a transcendent experience he had one night that radically altered the rest of his life. Others similarly gifted in science, simply by remaining faithful to their science, are finding more and more that the heart with its way of knowing is fact and, indeed, is all-pervasive. It's operative, say our physicists and chemists, in the least of the living beings such as bacteria, which have remarkable collective ways of intercommunication, and also in the most passive non-living matter such as the elusive photon, the smallest particle of light. As experiments continue to show, influences brought to bear on one of two identical photons affect the other, whatever the distance — a few miles or a hundred thousand — between them. An updated and expanded version of the ancient Chinese proverb: "The right man sitting in his house thinking the right thought will be heard five hundred miles away."

At root faith is this intuitive, spontaneous sort of knowledge transformed and elevated, enabling one to embrace with comfort and surety truths and actions that would otherwise be meaningless and irrational. This is why in the gospels faith is associated with miracles, the impossible — impossible, that is, to the purely rational mind. Can one born blind be made to see? Impossible, says the brain. But faith says yes and makes it happen (Jn 9). Can one dead be made to rise again? Absolutely not, says reason. Yet faith can make it happen (Jn 11). "My daughter, . . . your faith has restored you . . ." (Mk 5:34). "Everything is possible to one who has faith . . ." (Mk 9:23). "In truth I tell you, if your faith is the size of a mustard seed you will say to this mountain, 'Move from here to there,' and it will move, nothing will be impossible for you" (Mt 17:20).

And so I look on what appears to be a piece of bread and a cup of wine and I say "My Lord and my God," and mean it. My friend is waked, and I see in the casket only the dead shell of what she once was, yet I "know" beyond all visible evidence that she still lives — and more intensely than ever. I can't see, touch, taste God, and whenever I try to think of him my brain grows dizzy and I end in darkness and absurdity. Yet I know beyond knowing that he's here, there, everywhere, the soul of the soul of everything. I'm nothing to myself and from what I can see I'm not much to or for anyone else either, a sad waste of a man with little if any promising future. And yet under all my seeing and in spite of it I know I am of worth, I am loved, I am a precious gift of God to a world in need of me. Don't expect me to go into ecstasy over any of this, for I *feel* blessed little of it except maybe at rare moments — moments that seem to become rarer and rarer as I get older and older. But I do know the truth of it, for all my life, with its sins as well as its virtues, is centered upon it and issues from it. Before my knowing my being proclaims it. It is by faith that the just man lives (Rom 1:17). So does this unjust man, and this is his happiness.

Not that brain knowledge is of no use. Sure it is, and it's of a piece with faith. *Fides quaerens intellectum.* What a beautiful phrase out of antiquity: faith searching for understanding. It's a particular application of a broader "unified theory" antedating by centuries and surpassing the lesser theories of our quantum physicists: *Gratia perficit naturam.* The grace of God doesn't destroy but presupposes and perfects nature. Heaven and earth are in harmony. If you want to know about God, or at least something of him, then look to nature and look *with* nature, that is, with your native powers including reason. And if you want to know about the best of nature look with faith to the God who made and makes it. Faith and reason, science and revelation, body and spirit, love of God and love of God's world, all made one in a holy marriage in and through the union of the divine and the human in Christ.

But as with any marriage, this has to be worked at. Each must appreciate the worth of the other, trust the other, give the other space in which to move and grow, and help the other in the process. There'll be conflicts. How often my body aches against my spirit and my spirit against my body. How foolish faith may seem to reason and how lowly and unimportant my reason may appear to faith. Yet, what God has joined we must not divide. And every conflict is there simply that it might be worked through to a still deeper, faster union on the other side.

Since the dynamism of faith is toward understanding, faith doesn't eliminate or discourage questions; it raises them. It points reason in directions reason by itself can scarcely dream of, like some quiet voice within saying: Have you looked over here? What about this? Take a second look and a third. Why not try this? What's wrong with suffering? Have you really failed? Can't you be forgiven? What's God, *is* God? Who are you, why are you? What should you do with your life? The answers are already there in faith itself but they're unformed; they want the articulation of reason and of language. Like the instinct for food wants the eating of it, or like the inclination of love wants the visibility and tangibility of one who is loved.

So one who questions, and questions God himself, isn't one who lacks faith. Chances are such a one has it more deeply than someone who never questions. Even when no answers emerge or when they seem hostile to what one thought was believed, faith may still be there and all the stronger, searching for new, more vital articulation, egging reason on to creative thinking, urging the will to creative doing. Faith becomes incarnate in the world in which we live and becomes a maker of culture by being vital itself and keeping reason alive and hungry for present as well as past truth. Faith by itself, comfortably enclosed and guarded within, isn't faith at all but illusion. Faith must embrace reason, her spouse, and so beget the world. But always she is the dear one, the deep one, and our reason is to find its home in her, however dark and unsettling that home may be from time to time.

Faith, *my* faith, is broader and deeper than my individual heart. It's within me whispering, sometimes shouting, what it wants of me and stirring me to act accordingly. But it's also outside and all around me, in other people and other things. The whispering and shouting find their echo in other hearts and sometimes originate there.

Which is to say that faith is a communal affair. "For where two or three meet in my name, I am there among them" (Mt 18:20). Need we be gathered together *explicitly* in his name for faith to be at work? "The wind blows where it pleases . . . So it is with everyone who is born of the Spirit" (Jn 3:8). Faith overspills me and others, creating an atmosphere, a presence, an ocean in which we are meant to live and move together.

So I listen for God not just within but also outside me, and know that others, whether they're aware of it or not, are listening for him in me. "Deep is calling to deep by the roar of your cataracts" (Ps 42:7). In spite of all the noise on the surface of things, the bedlam, confusion, division, sin, hostility — the *lack* of community — under it all, in the depth of it all, that "still, small voice" is within, reminding us that we are of the one Father-Mother God and so are meant to be one with and for one another. It doesn't always work out this way, of course. We're too much on the surface and hear only the roaring of the surf and the cry of the gull. But now and again we're drawn below and forced to listen to the silence. How beautiful this can be, but also how terrible. "O dark, dark, dark, they all go into the dark . . ." But no matter one way or the other as long as sometime before the end we learn to live or try to live within our common faith.

"Let's not just sit here. Let's walk along the beach."

Earlier, at her apartment, it was the same thing. "Can't we go somewhere? I'm afraid . . ." So they had gotten into her bright new yellow Pinto and driven the few miles to the ocean. "Beautiful," she said as she braked and opened the door. She walked round to the back, lifted the hatch and rummaged. He sat there, staring straight ahead at the leaden sky and ocean. But he felt her behind him, rummaging. She closed the hatch. "Let's go."

He followed her down the steep rocky path onto the sand. The beach was desolate — only a few scattered people and a couple of dogs far down along the crescent. He walked behind her for a while and then she let him catch up. "Strange, there are no shells on this beach." He looked. She was right. Hadn't he noticed that before? Often he had come here, to think his sermons and lectures through, correct papers, pray, or simply be mesmerized into oblivion by sight and sound of the ocean. He must have noticed. But now, as if for the first time, he saw how clean and smooth the beach was. Only — if you looked closely — a solitary shell or stone here and there, a bottle half-buried in the sand, a small fragment of driftwood. All scarcely visible in the long stretch of slick curving sand and water.

They walked in silence for what seemed to him a long time. They passed, and left behind, a young couple huddled together talking and laughing and trying to make their playful, yapping bulldog pup behave. Then he wandered up from the tide line onto the dry sand and sat down. The woman followed and sat by him, a little forward and at arm's length. "Do you want to read my book?" He said no, and lay back, while she, upright like an ancient Buddha, sat there and read.

The sky was clearing now, and soon it was all a deep transparent blue. The morning sun was far up, almost overhead, and out to the west hung a faint half-moon, looking still and shy, like a displaced dream — one come too early or too late. He pointed the moon out to her and asked why only half. An idle, stupid question, he realized, but they had been courting inanities all morning. At least she was, and he, though disinclined, was playing her game. "I don't know. Maybe the other half got lost. Or maybe it was swallowed up by one of those airish beasts Plato talks about." "You should ask Jimmy," he ventured. Jimmy was her six-year-old son. "He studies that kind of thing in school, doesn't he?" She laughed and said she'd ask him. "Jim knows all kinds of interesting things now. Probably even knows the size of the moon — even when it's full!" Clever, witty girl. She laughed again, then settled back into her book.

He turned over on his stomach and observed the sand. It was warm but still damp and pockmarked, and minute bugs and flies were busily managing their little lives, blithely unaware of the god watching them. Below the surface of his mind he was thinking of his own God watching him, always watching him. He lay his head down on his arm and tried to sleep off his drowsiness. No luck. He sat up and moved forward just a fraction, his eyes fixed on the woman's soft brown hair and rounded shoulders. So beautiful, he felt, and so right, there in the context of white sand and gray-green ocean and infinite sky. He wanted to reach out and touch her, hold her. But he knew she would either stiffen or yield indifferently, coldly. She desired him — he felt sure of that — but she would not surrender herself to him. She was afraid, for herself and for him. She had once given herself to another and made a mess of things. Her Jimmy was the only happy result. No marriage, not even a proper affair. A few passionate meetings, some vague plans, and it was over, with contempt and hatred on either side. Now she feared love and still felt her shame. "I don't want to drag you down to my level," she had once cried out as she turned from him. Humiliated, angered, he told her to "cut that crap out." "Anyway," she continued, "I don't want that kind of relationship with you. I need you for something more. Please, just friends, just special friends."

Something more. It was there from the beginning. He knew it and scrupulously tried to do it justice. But there was the other thing too, and now and again it would surface in spite of efforts to keep it down. Like that first time years ago when, still a romantic, girlish college student, all excited she came to him with a dream she had had of him. She liked it, she said, because it held two of her favorite kinds of people — dogs and him! She dreamt she was in lovely sunny country and as she walked through it she came upon a high and gentle hill all covered with green and yellow grass; and on top of the hill was a little cottage in which *he* dwelt. Around the bottom of the hill were playful little dogs that welcomed and fawned upon everyone who would climb the hill. But halfway up were other larger dogs who would let pass only a few who were his closest friends. But on the very top of the hill surrounding the cottage were huge dogs, quiet but fierce and firm, who would allow no one to enter.

He told her he liked the dream too, though it saddened him some. Then, with a smile, he added that he didn't know whether the dogs were there to keep others out or himself in! Her eyes filled. He laughed and said there was no cause for tears. It was better this way. But something deep within their friendship was disturbed in that brief moment, and both of them were aware of it.

She graduated, they said a tentative goodbye. Occasionally they would meet and talk, in friendship; and he helped her along as she fell in love and crashed out of it. A year or two of silence, and then the letter that broke it. She apologized and explained that her silence was because of the guilt she felt over her love for him: "I want from you a love that I know a priest can't give." It all returned to him — his fondness for her, his own love for her. He was stirred and excited, more now than ever before, for in the meantime the tide of loneliness had risen within him, and he ached for intimacy. He wrote and told her not to worry: "God would provide and prevent." Disappointingly he was being proved right. Their half-formed hopes made little difference. God, as usual, was having his way. They were in suspension, slowly, absurdly dancing round each other, afraid even to raise their eyes because of what they might see.

He was tired now. He didn't want to go on like this. He couldn't make love to her, he knew, even if she were willing. He might go through the motions, even bring it off physically; but his spirit, his love — just as she had once dreamed — would be locked within. He and the woman would forever remain on either side of the wall — of God. Somehow it was like that vast expanse of sky and ocean, and ghostly half-moon. Their love was at once too big for them and too small. As years ago on his ordination day when he stole away to the ocean and stood on the edge of the cliff and looked out over the late evening sky and the darkening waters. He had often stood there and felt so small — a frail, brief atom in an endless universe. But now with his ordination it was different. He had magnitude within him — the power and the love to change mere creation into the Creator himself. "This is my body . . ." If the ocean and sky were still immense he was no longer small; and from that day forward he knew that no merely human love could ever contain him. It seemed to be the same with her, but because of another kind of baptism. All her pain and shame in love, the young hope she had had in it, and the despair. Love was no longer enough for her, not nearly enough, and passion only an uncomfortable itching of the skin. Apart, each of them might dream of surrender, even hope and plan for it, but face to face the dream dissolved. The immensity within dwarfed the vastness of possible love.

He stood up and headed back to the car. She followed, at a distance, stopping now and again for a lone shell or stone, "for Jimmy." The rest of the early afternoon they spent driving up the coast and down along the skyline back to the apartment. There his blood ran warm again, but nothing came of it. She had to go, she said, to pick up Jimmy at school; maybe they could get together again next week "for another outing." Some weeks later he tried to recall what he said and did then, but couldn't. He remembered only the awareness that it was over between them even though it had scarcely begun.

Off and on through the next ten years he had news of her but nothing worth remembering until the last announcement. She had died, he was told, over a year ago. It was a gradual death. First the cancer ate her breasts, then her womb, then everything. God (*goddamned God!*) had finally taken her, as they say. But he had taken her long since, he knew; as he had taken almost everything that was his, or nearly his. It took him some time to recover from the shock and depression of her death, but in the press of other concerns he gradually forgot about her, though not entirely. Now and again, quite unexpectedly and without any visible reason — at Mass, while he was preaching, at a party, on the edge of sleep or deep within it — a solitary, unvarying image of her would flash before him and as suddenly vanish. It was of her back to him on white sand against the eternal gray of the ocean, a thin, frail Buddha under a silent heaven.

TWO

In the Beginning, God

I think, Lord, of your immensity. Before anything was those billions of years ago, you *are*; and if everything should cease to be, you will remain, and not in lonely isolation, but complete, in fullness of love and joy within yourself, living that ineffable communal life we feebly, haltingly call Father, Son, and Holy Spirit. You're above all, beyond all. You're beyond the material universe. Where is that farthest galaxy, that most distant star? You're far beyond and above it. You're beyond all that is of mind and spirit: our highest thought and deepest love barely touch the surface of all you are, and they are able to do thus much only because you yourself have first touched and raised them to you.

Yet how intimate to all! I can't stop proclaiming it. With your saints I want to shout it out, sing it to the world. You're the stone within the stone, the silence within the heart of silence. You're the ultimate depth of every ocean, the smallest particle of every atom, the inmost cell of every drop of blood, the gene within the gene determining what, who we are, the throbbing core of every loving (and unloving) heart. You're the Self within myself, the still point of the turning world, and the tingling wire that strings it all together. And on and on and on. You're so marvelously intimate to all *because* you're so much above all. Like the artist who does his best work, enters most deeply and vitally into his creation, in the times he transcends his art. Like the lover who loves most profoundly and fiercely when she rises above all limitations of human love. Like those who do most for the world when they stand above it and so find leverage to raise it higher. Beyondness and intimacy are not opposed. They're interconnected, and at the level of God they are one and the same.

So it is that you became one of us, flesh of our flesh. Your immensity all but compelled you to create a universe vast and infinite as yourself and to act in love at the heart of all of it. But this was still too small a thing for you. You had to *become* your own creation, so that now you are not only at the heart of each baby, present and loving in its every cry and gurgle, but you *are* a baby born in lowliness, a little child growing up with other children, a young adult carving wood and fitting it together piece by piece, a teacher, a doctor, one living for the truth and finally dying for it — and for all of us. Again, no contradiction here, simply the ultimate term of a love so immense that it must become that which it loves.

Now and again in graced moments — times when I break away — I glimpse something of the truth of this. When I go off into some desert or onto some mountain top or stand alone by some ocean or when I'm immersed in the stillness of prayer — whenever, that is, I get away from the world, I find I can look back upon it and see more of it and more deeply into it, and love it the more, than when I'm smack up against it. When I stand back from one I love — when, as the poet says, I let spaces be in our togetherness — I see her more clearly, more deeply, and love her the more intimately for it. It's as that funny little song has it: "How'm I gonna miss ya if ya don't go away?" All true love not only wants to be with the other but to become the other. But the only way to do this, and do it right, is at the same time to stand above, and stand free.

My dear God, let me see more and more how great your love is and therefore how little you have become because of it, and how much a glad servant of all that you have made. Let me always strive after your immensity that I too, in my own measure, might become one, intimately one, with your creation and serve it in your kind of love.

Somerset Maugham published a novel in 1943 that helped popularize far eastern religions in the western world. The novel, *The Razor's Edge* (a phrase out of the Hindu *Upanishads*), was immediately made into a fine film that did even more to enhance the popularity of Hindu and Buddhist religions throughout Europe and America. The story tells of a young man discontented with his native Christianity and the superficiality of life within and around him. He travels east in search of the truth. In India, by the grace of a holy guru and a mystical experience, he finds it. He returns to his former world transformed. He's wise, disciplined, deeply at peace within himself and with others. By word and deed he amazes and unsettles old friends still trapped in the materialism and surface Christianity from which he has escaped.

At one point in the novel he explains why he rejected Christianity in favor of eastern religion. He says that he could not accept a tyrannical God who required his subjects to bow down before him in worship. "I myself think," he declares, "that the need to worship is no more than the survival of an old remembrance of cruel gods that had to be propitiated." In other words, in Christianity you become a slave of God, constantly having to look up and bow down to him, whereas — such is the implication — in the east you *become* God.

One might answer that the young man was being rather unfair and shallow in his judgment. He was comparing the ideal of eastern religion as seriously lived with Christianity as so often debased by those who are Christian in name only. If he had looked to the great Christian mystics and saints and to many lesser folk who truly loved Jesus, and then matched this realized ideal with millions of superficially religious easterners, his judgment might have been reversed. He would have seen the latter as the slaves of a hundred tyrannical gods and the Christians as free in the spaciousness of the divine within and all around them.

True Christian worship is not so much a matter of bowing down to God as opening up to him. It's the response to the realization that we are incomplete, that just as we hunger and thirst for food, drink, affection, knowledge, and love, so something still deeper in us longs to be raised to where we can see and live beyond ourselves. This looking beyond to a higher dimension and wanting to be lifted to it constitutes Christian worship as it's meant to be. In the gospel of John Jesus prays for his disciples at their last gathering: "May they all be one, just as, Father, you are in me and I am in you, so that they also may be in us,. . . that they may be one as we are one. With me in them and you in me, may they be so perfected in unity" (Jn 17:21-23). The operative words here are *in* and *one*: We are to be *in* Jesus, *in* the Father, and they *in* us. Our limited human, often inhuman, life is to be taken up *into* the limitless, spacious life of God — one free humanly divine, divinely human life for all of us. If we don't reach above and beyond ourselves in true worship then we will search beneath ourselves for what we think will complete us. Thus we will become smaller and smaller and eventually shrivel up and die, not just in body but, what is much worse, in mind and spirit. So the frustrated, a-religious psychiatrist in Peter Schaffer's *Equus*: "Without worship, you shrink."

And is it, after all, so bad now and again to bow down before God and want to be his servant? On the contrary, there's something rather beautiful about this. There must be, since God himself stooped to our level: He emptied himself, says St. Paul, to become one of us and *our* servant. And there at the Last Supper he knelt down before his disciples and washed their feet before going out and dying in a paroxysm of worship of us. In worship, it seems, God rather bows down to us than we to him. Yes, right and beautiful it is to be able to look up, to God and to others. The terrible thing is to have nowhere to look but down.

A basic concern is the question of reality. What's real, what's unreal? What's authentic, inauthentic? What's true, false, genuine, phoney? What's superficial and fleeting, what's deep and lasting?

I go on retreat, away from my everyday world. At first it all seems unreal, foreign, a mere respite from the things of home. After the second, third, fourth day *this* begins to be home and that other place some foreign land I used to inhabit. I see things I never saw before except maybe fleetingly. My feelings change, my heart slows down, I feel calm and at peace. God and the things of God make sense now. They're real. And what of that other world I had just come from? Illusion, unreal, a sad waste of the gift of life. But once back, it's not long before it becomes my reality once again and the retreat a pleasant but illusory dream.

Sunday worship must be unreal for so many. They measure their daily life, their real world, against what the minister is saying and doing and they wonder, if only unconsciously, what all this has to do with them, their family, their work, their play. And the minister, looking out over that same congregation, wonders why they don't see what he does and live accordingly, or, sadly, why *he* doesn't see what they do and so himself change from illusion to reality.

When one is young certain things seem real that become unreal with age. When one is alone and out of love reality is much different than when love strikes and a new world opens up. A drug addict's reality is different from a nun's, a revolutionary's from a hermit's, the poor person's from the rich. Where is the real, if anywhere?

Is it perhaps that all is real but on different levels, and that each level is continuous with the next? Only when the different levels are isolated one from the other, and when their innate hierarchical order is disrupted, does unreality set in. Thus I look to the God of my faith and find him to be the highest reality, *ens realissimum* as St. Thomas expresses it. Next in the order of reality is the human Jesus most intimately continuous with the God he *is*. Then the woman Mary continuous with Christ human and divine, and finally in ordered succession the rest of creation from angels to ants and below — the great chain of being that the medieval world affirmed. The modern world, whether of the sciences or the arts or plain old raw experience, presupposes, often in spite of itself, and tries to maintain this same order. Where it has been lost, there's a longing to restore it.

Levels of reality, one leading into the other — and so the poet writes a poem and it's good, true, real because it's part of him, says something of what's alive in him. He writes another that grows out of the experience of the first but holds more of him. He writes another and another, each one, if he's lucky, more "real" than the preceding until he writes the greatest of all because it's all of him, the fullness of his life. Here, at last, is reality for him. Not that all the rest are unreal now, except maybe by comparison. Each poem led into the next and helped make it possible. It's the totality that's real, but also each of the parts singly as it engendered and enters into the master work.

And so the poet God. The least of his work appears in the beginning — a chaotic mass of whatever; then the seas and the earth — fine poems; the fishes and the plants — still better; the birds and the animals, all climaxing in that great poem, the human being. Finally the finest song of all, God's perfect work: his own Son conceived by the Spirit and birthed by Mary. And all is real insofar as it led up to this perfect work and is held within it, helped prepare for it and now is part of and reflects it. All creation is real because it belongs to Christ and Christ to God.

The lover says to his beloved: "I love you for your lips and eyes and hair." She answers, "Fine, but is there more?" He says, "I love you for your scintillating personality." And she responds, "How very nice, and is there more?" He says, "I love you for your own tender, gentle love and all your goodness." And she, "That's better still, but is there not something more?" He thinks it over, looks deeply into her clear, honest eyes and ventures, "I love you for the God who is within you — who *is* you in your heart of hearts." And she, "Thanks for that. Now you have all of me, now and forever."

In the same way, I'm to love my body and all that it is and can do. It's real and so the love of it is real. I'm to love my mind, the greater thing it is and greater things it can do. Here is fuller, richer reality. I'm to love my spirit, its rootedness in God, it's oneness with God when I'm right with him. Here's my greatest reality. All the rest is true and real as it moves into this, and this is true and real as it embraces all the rest. I'm to love myself down to my very ground, which is God. And thus shall I love others as myself: up on the surface where they visibly dance and sing, joy and sorrow, where they're lovely like spring or worn and wasted like winter, but always my love will move to where God is in them and where all else is made and kept real.

Here is context once again. Not things, people, systems, institutions in isolation, but all organic parts of a vital whole. Happiness is a matter of vision. "He who can see far enough is not unhappy," says the poet. This is why we're so unhappy, then. We can see far with our physical eyes — far out into distant galaxies and deep into gyrating atomic particles. But the eyes of our minds, our spirits? How confined and myopic! Many today are afraid of vision. *What* will they see once the spirit's released? They're so used to the dark that they're afraid of the light. They've seen only pieces of life separated from other pieces; but this is death, like my head severed from the rest of my body. They think of context as only all the dead pieces added together which, of course, can mean only greater death, multiplied death, absolute death. But to see each thing as alive, not just with its own life but with that of all else, is to find that it all adds up to the fullness of life wherein death has no hold. What's to fear, then, from letting our inward vision sweep the universe and view it as does the kindly God who made it?

So at the moment I'm searching my special calling. What's the value, the sense, of my religious life? If I look at only one or several of the particulars of it — my vows, my worship, my ministry, my living in a community of men — I can become quite sad, especially as I see them only in context of the particulars of other people's lives or of the media's depiction of those lives. I compare and contrast and more often than not I find my life wanting, unreal: All the propaganda is in favor of the reality of the way of the world. But if I look deeply into the vital connectedness of my vows, worship, community, and ministry and see it relative to the needs, both silent and vocal, of the world — if I see, that is, my life as a necessary and organic part of the lives of others even when they don't — then reality is on my side as much as, if not more than, theirs. I read the papers, I see the films, I hear the laughter and the cries of pain, but I read, see, hear between the lines, where my life fits in. The world's children and God's, in their deepest hearts, become my context as, I hope, my life becomes theirs. Not several lives now but one, and all is real.

Help me, Lord, to see my life whole and as one with others as well as with you. I want to appreciate this body of mine in spite of the nuisance and snare it so often is to me and to others. It's of a piece with the rest of me and as such I want to love it.

I want to appreciate and use well my mind. It's a good one, not brilliant certainly, but careful, persistent, sometimes imaginative, hungry for the true and the beautiful. But it tends to get tired and discouraged and sometimes it distorts and lies, and then I begin to hate and give up on it. Guard me from this.

I especially want to cherish my spirit with all the Spirit's gifts — faith, hope, love, fortitude, prudence, justice, temperance, wisdom, understanding and all the rest. Your very life is at that center where I most am. It's all there but so often dormant, or rather I'm dormant to it. Wake me up. Help me to see all I am and live accordingly.

Help me to enter into the lives of others. Not as a boor and a busybody, but silently, unobtrusively. First by prayer, the kind of prayer that makes others' lives mine so that my cry for them *de profundis* is their very own for themselves. Of themselves they might not want you, but with my prayer within them they now may find themselves longing for you and your love. Secondly, by doing for them in ways that they don't suspect. I don't want to be a do-gooder, a revolutionary on behalf of the poor, a public advocate of the rights of minorities. . . this for others, but for me no, unless, of course, you want it so. I'd like, rather, to do things quietly — unnoticed in my lifetime and forever thereafter.

Help me to let others enter into my life. I would like to love, but I would like also to be loved, for my sake but also for the sake of those who need to give love but find no welcoming heart to receive it. With them as with myself I want love to keep on the move, sinking ever more deeply till it reaches you and then moving further and further into you, till you are all in all — not apart from all, but *in* all. Don't let me put a halt to love and so spoil it, for myself and others.

Here context is indeed everything. It's community in all its depth and breadth, the living mystical body of Christ, the realization of St. Augustine's strange prediction: "In the end there will be one Christ in love with himself." Heavy stuff, Lord, and who can manage it? Let me at least make a beginning not too far from the end.

Even though it's some twenty years since he left, I still feel sad when I think of N's parting words: "I love God, I love people, I love my guitar. But I hate religion." It was in the quixotic sixties. He had functioned as a priest for only a short time. He seemed to be doing well. People, especially the young, liked him, his liturgies, his preaching, his music. Then it all came tumbling down. His goodbyes were complete and final.

What did religion mean to him? What, I suppose, it's meant to many through the ages: mere formality — external gesture with no internal roots; hypocrisy — the whitened sepulcher filled with dead men's bones; cruelty — from human blood sacrifice to crusade to inquisition to mental and moral torture; soporific drug — to lull the poor into accepting the injustices of the rich in the false hope of finding justice hereafter; illusion and cowardice — to escape the pain, anguish and loneliness endemic to life as it *really* is; deceit — to fill the pockets of the preacher and the coffers of the church.

The pity is that so much of this is true. Who having read history and been alert to current events can gainsay it? But it's only half the picture and probably the lesser half. If we look more closely, read between the lines and lives I think another more positive picture is in evidence. Certainly there are the saints, holy ones of both east and west who give the lie to such an exclusive account. They're human and humanly vulnerable and flawed, and are the first to confess it, but overall they're a people of remarkable sanity, whose worship springs from the joy, pain, and love of their hearts, who are alive to life, who strive for justice especially for the poor, who are creative of others, who deliberately go in want that others might have, who face the pain and loneliness of life and move in and through it to the love and joy on the other side. The litanies could be endless: Moses, Homer, Buddha, Christ, Paul, Augustine...Francis, Dominic, Aquinas, Catherine, Teresa...Damien, Gandhi, Dorothy Day, Mother Teresa, Martin Luther King, Jr.... and thousands upon thousands in between. These are the great ones, the shapers of civilization and cultures. But think of all the little unnoticed ones who have reached sanity in and through religion, who instead of surrendering to the bleakness of life have searched for and found its goodness and left their little patch of world better than they found it.

In any event, however badly one might think of religion it's unavoidable. In this, it's a lot like love. Think of how tragic love can be and has been: all the horror of it, the murders committed because of it, the suicides, the mental anguish and physical pain, the crippling of children. It may often be true, as the poet suggests, that "each man kills the thing he loves," yet we don't advocate doing away with love. We still agree it's the best that we have; at least we cynically admit that though we might not be able to live with it we can't live without it. It's the same with religion. It's as strong an appetite in us as that for food and drink and sex — even stronger. It's a metaphysical thing. Easier to escape ourselves than it. We might abandon one form of religion but immediately we're caught up in another. We might give up on the Mass and then find ourselves religiously in awe at a seance or wildly alive at a baseball game. We might reject the pope and his authority and then find ourselves grovelling before a Hitler or a Stalin, or quoting some guru or theologian as though he were scripture itself. Ritual, sacred or secular, has tenacious hold on us. And rather than being the cause of neuroses and insanity as our most notorious psychologist claimed, such sickness is more the result of the loss of religion and ritual, as his greatest pupil insisted.

Religion is the essential attitude of the creature to the Creator. We all know ourselves as creature: We emerge out of nothing and of ourselves we tend back into nothing. Here is the ultimate source of our fear and anguish, as the existentialists were so good at highlighting: We stand on the edge of the abyss and are always just about to fall. But when we turn from the awareness of our nothingness to the One who brings and holds us from it then we have religion. The point of our nothingness turns out to be that still point of God, and so we begin our worship. "You are the one who is," said St. Catherine to the Lord, "I am the one who is not." Where nothingness and Being meet, there is religion.

But for religion to be true and not deviate into what Father N and so many others have reckoned, it has to be guarded and its wholeness observed — like love itself.

God must be worshipped as both transcendent and immanent, above all but also within all. If he's worshipped only as transcendent then we lose the sense of the worth of this world, we are less disinclined to waste and sacrifice the world and the people within it for life beyond it. If we worship God only as immanent then this life becomes everything, the sacred is reduced to the secular; instead of God being in the world, the world itself becomes God. The world, then, stands under no higher judgment — and can be raised to no higher level. With no source of inspiration and energy outside itself it can only turn inward upon itself, shrink, and die, and we along with it.

God must be seen as end not means. God is for us, as amply demonstrated in the life, death, and resurrection of Jesus, but only because we are first and last for him. He is our happiness, not ourselves, and he would have us remember this. But so often, and often in subtle, almost unconscious ways, we reverse the process, to our loss and misery. We use God to inspire fear or guilt (as with children or parishioners), or anger (as in a "holy war" or violent protest) in order to have our own way. I preach God (or write about him) to swell my ego and fill my pocketbook. I become and remain a religious for my security and little pleasures. Thus my worship becomes worship not of God but myself. Instead of opening up and out to what's greater than I and thereby becoming greater myself, I close in on myself and so vanish into the nothingness whence I came.

My worship of God must be total. It must involve all of me and reach out to all. "You must love the Lord your God with all your heart, with all your soul, and with all your mind. . . . You must love your neighbor as yourself" (Mt 22:37). If God is transcendent I worship him in mystery, that is, in all I don't and can't know. If he's immanent I worship him down to the last atom of the universe, and with everything I am: my body ("With my body I do thee worship"), my imagination (art, music, poetry), my memory (history, prayer of remembrance), my head (science, math, philosophy, theology), my heart (faith and love). Wherever religion is restrictive of the human beware of it. We must always distinguish the human from the inhuman, from that which may seem human but is in reality destructive of it. But we must be equally careful to recognize and advance the truly human and make it into our total worship of God.

I must approach my God in humility and trust: Humility, because I know I am from nothing and if left to myself will tumble back into nothing; trust, because I know even better that the God who made me out of his love will keep me in

his love. I may fluctuate from one to the other. I may have
my days, years of fear and guilt when I'm able to see little
if anything beyond my self and the black hole at its center. I
may have my times of confidence and joyful abandon when I
seem to see only God. But most of the time I'll be somewhere
in between. But whatever the case I must continually hold to
both humility and trust. "I am the one who is not," and so,
Lord, I cry to you out of the depth of my nothingness; "You
are the one who is," and so I trust that in your love for me
you will not let me go.

Religion lies at the heart of all of us, in some more, in
some less. But there are specialists in religion, those who
make it their lifelong concern to live it, study its dynamic,
put it into words and acts, and so keep it visibly alive for the
people of God. Others may be holier than they, may feel more
profoundly the cry for God within them and hear more sharply
God's cry for them, and may live lives more in accord with
their belief. But precisely because they are so deeply religious
they long for those who have the time, energy, intelligence,
learning, love, in short *vocation*, to make visible for them the
invisible, to give them words and gestures that might express,
if only feebly, their deepest desires and keep their love alive,
healthy, and constantly moving into God. Accordingly, they
make for themselves and accept priests and ministers of the
Lord.

All are meant to be priests and ministers in one sense or
another. All of us, said St. Paul, one of the earliest Christian
priests, are to minister to each other according to our particular gifts. But within this general ministration there are those
drawn apart, as Shamans, Levites, as Jesus himself and his
chosen twelve, who have nothing else to do but continually
strive to make God visible that the rest of us might find the

way into the richness of his invisibilty and mystery, here as well as hereafter.

For Christianity there is but one priest. Jesus Christ by his word and deed became the way, truth, and life, our bridge between heaven and earth, the visibility of God. But his word and deed had to be extended into every time and place, kept alive before the people that they might in their own lifetime be witness to it and enabled to enter into it. Those among us who bear the title of priest are presenters of Jesus, speakers and showers of Jesus' word and deed, not their own.

This is crucial to Christian faith. Christian priests need not, as priests, be healers, eloquent of truth, heroic in action. They need not be saints. Rather than be seen, they are to be seen through, and if there is to be anything heroic about their lives it is to be in the self-effacement that allows Christ to be manifest. This is why primarily priesthood is and has always been a matter of ritual, a making present of the divine *Other*, who in the instance of Christian priesthood, is Jesus Christ. It is the priest's job to make clear to the people, as to himself, that it is not he or any other merely human being who saves but the divine and human Jesus Christ.

Christian ritual, however, isn't simply a matter of formal word and gesture. It is also the vital entering into the ritual, the completion of it in the priest's and people's own subsequent action and passion. The ritual sacraments are to be performed only that they might be lived. Through sacramental signs, Christ enters into our lives that we might enter into his life and be of help to each other in remaining there.

One week ago Father John was made a servant of the people of God. Not a master of God's people, having power to command and force, but one after the heart of the master of all of us who said to his disciples the very night he made them priests: "Among the gentiles, it is the kings who lord it

over them . . . yet here am I among you as one who serves"
(Lk 22:27).

Put quite simply, John's service will consist in providing
for the sacramental life of the church. He will baptize, absolve,
offer the Holy Sacrifice and give communion; he will anoint
the sick and the dying; he will bless marriages, sometimes
confirm, and perhaps he might even one day ordain others to
the priesthood. This is his province, his service. He is now a
man of religion and of ritual.

But precisely for this reason, he is a man of life and of
living. Religion is no category set off from others, a specialty
unto itself. It enters into every space and hidden corner of
our life. The very air we breathe is God's, and so a matter
of religion; the beating of our heart is God's beating against
our own and so a matter of ritual. Even in those dark areas
where people deliberately try to forget or reject God, still
he is present, at least in shadow, and so there is religion.
Someone has said that our life is haunted by transcendence.
Yes, everywhere we go, in everything we do, there is the
presence of God, and so there is religion.

The priest, then, mediating *life* between God and people
stands at the heart of it all. When he baptizes, it isn't simply
that he pours water and says some ancient formula. No, in
baptizing he stands at the very beginning of a human life,
not just its supernatural life, but the whole of its life: eating,
drinking, sleeping, loving, hating, seeing, hearing, thinking,
playing. The entire person is washed to the core by the hand
and word of the priest. Nothing, absolutely nothing is the same
once he places us, newly born in Christ, in the arms of our
Father.

But that's not all. His influence over the baptized doesn't
stop with pouring the water and anointing with chrism. He has
the right and duty now to enter into their lives, to help keep
them fresh and innocent, receptive to all the life and beauty

that sings around and within them. He must see to it that they *remain* God's children forever.

After he's offered the eucharist, Christ's redeeming act, and fed us with Christ's body he must go on feeding us. He must try to keep us aware that we are redeemed in *every* moment by the blood of Christ; that we are always "oned" to Christ in love; that we are all sisters and brothers in our Father's house meant to eat our fill at a *common* table. Yes, when the priest feeds us with Christ's body that's the beginning of his continually feeding us with Christ's truth. "And the Word was made flesh . . . " Christ's word and his flesh go together.

When in Christ's name he forgives in the dark or light of the confessional it's the sign as well as the consummation of his daily work of mercy: trying to convince us that sins sorrowed for, God not only forgives but forgets; encouraging us also to forgive and forget sins committed against ourselves; laboring to prevent sin and all the sickness of mind and heart that comes from it by creating an atmosphere of understanding and love and beauty; making up in his own flesh and spirit for the crimes of humanity.

Blessing marriage is his key to the Christian home. How he must labor for its preservation! No easy task, especially in our time, to bring people to an awareness of a human love that embraces the flesh surely, but reaches deep into the spirit; a human love that reverences, worships the divine in the other, that isn't only for possession but for surrender and sacrifice, that doesn't kill or limit life but creates it, that's alert to the sophistries of those who have lost the sacrament of human love and so have lost human love itself.

When he anoints the sick and the dying then he, the priest, becomes most aware of how very true it is that he has been ordained to bring life. He doesn't anoint just to restore health of body and/or prepare the dying for the world to come. He must continually try, in whatever ways he can, to help bring the poor body of this world along. He must, alone and with others, feed the hungry, give drink to the thirsty, clothe the naked, visit the sick and imprisoned, shelter the homeless, always aware of the great and shocking truth of Christianity: The body itself is meant to live and live forever, and so even now merits our deep respect and reverence and religious care.

This life-bearing service will come relatively easy to Father John because I think he was born with an exceptional gift for life. He loves people — loves to be with them, make them happy, make them laugh. He has a gift and a passion for the spoken word, a gift for engagement and dialogue. He loves the beauty in art and literature and drama, and especially in drama he has creative gifts. As a Dominican he's come a long way in his devotion to truth and his appreciation for right and full and balanced thinking. As a religious he's gotten to know his God and what eternal life is about, and to hold Christ as his friend. No, he'll not be tempted as much as others simply to administer the sacraments. By God's special grace fulfilling his own natural gifts his ritual will bring life to God's people and continually broaden and deepen his own.

Prayer, like religion, is both necessary and primal. It is preparation for action and suffering: prayer of petition, in which we ask God for favors, especially the grace to act right and be able to suffer with proper will, but also contemplative prayer, that we might become empty, a clean channel for God's act and God's suffering. Contemplative prayer is itself needed for prayer of petition: that we might ask for what's right, or rather, let the Spirit ask within and for us. It seems everybody prays, in one form or another, at one time or another. Especially in times of crisis, times of pain, we cry out to something or someone beyond us who we think can help. The primitives did and do it, the urbane of our or any age do it. Even the atheist, I venture, at times would at least like to pray and even, at times, has to swallow a cry for God surging within in order to remain consistent with treasured disbelief.

The freudian response, of course, is that prayer is simply a continuation and extention of childhood reliance on one's parents. When we are children they are the almighty ones who are there with their help and gifts at our beseeching. As we grow older something of the child remains within us while the power of our parents recedes. We construct, then, a new father and mother to match our need and cry to them, or, hopeless, we merely suffer the cry to emerge and spend itself in the dark and the void.

But it seems to me that St. Paul has a better, or at least equally valid, response: the parenthood of God *precedes* that of our natural parents, names it, and is the very real subject/object of our prayer: "This, then, is what I pray, kneeling before the Father, from whom every fatherhood, in heaven or on earth, takes its name. In the abundance of his glory may he, through his Spirit, enable you to grow firm in power with regard to your inner self" (Eph 3:14-16). Our first cry, even as we emerge from our mother's womb, is for God, and, at bottom, every other cry in our lifetime is also for him.

Why do we pray, seeing that God, being God, knows what we want before we even begin to think of what we want? The first reason is implied above. We pray because we have to. As creatures, that is, out of nothing and of ourselves tending back into nothing, our whole being reaches out to the One who sustains us in being. Praying, like the rest of religion, is a metaphysical thing. Not just we ourselves in our conscious minds pray, but the Spirit deep within us cries out "Abba!" ("Father") (cf. Gal 4:6). But our conscious praying, that which we ourselves formulate for definite things and people, has its reasons.

First, not so much that we might inform God as to what we want, but that we ourselves might come to know what we want and in God's light judge whether or not it's right for us. Often our desires are fixed on things that are harmful, for us and for others, and we don't know it. "If I had only known!" "I didn't know what I was doing!" Infamous last words. But to bring our hearts before God who is truth and there speak our desires is to be less liable to mistake the bad for the good and more likely to direct ourselves and others in the way of truth.

A second reason for praying is that we might become more and more aware that "all that is good, all that is perfect, is given us from above; it comes down from the Father of all light" (Jas 1:16). We seldom reflect on this truth. We take it for granted that *we* are the givers or that good things as well as bad come only by luck or chance. In prayer we at least allow for the possibility that God has something to do not just with the universe in general but with me and my least desires here and now. Our prayer becomes, as it were, a key that unlocks the universe allowing God to enter in and be the personal and lavish giver he longs to be.

Yet another reason is that we might come to better appreciate what and whom we pray for. Concentrating on them as worthy of God's love and care we see them as deserving from us too precisely the kind of caring love that God himself has for them. We are so used to thinking of things and people as being for us: Our parents are for us, our friends are for us, the sun and moon and stars, the rivers, lakes, oceans, the animals, fish, birds . . . all are for us. But praying for them reminds me that I am also for them, they have a claim upon me. So I am for my parents, my husband, wife, children, friends; I am for the sun and moon and stars. I am the servant of the rivers, lakes, oceans, my dog or my cat. The world is given into my hands for my use and need and pleasure. But I am also given to the world to reverence it and care for it and even, if need be, lay down my life for it. It is prayer that begins to teach me such an essential and life giving truth.

But prayer, if it be right and full, does not terminate in the things of the world and does much more than secure and add to our appreciation of them. As it begins with God — our calling upon him — so it is meant to end with him. First I think of God and call out to him. Then I offer him the things or people I'm concerned with, placing my petition before him. But if my prayer is genuine I find myself little by little forgetting the thing I'm asking for and remembering more and more the God whom I'm addressing. Or rather, I begin to see him as the heart and soul of my concern, the best of what or whom my prayer is for. The object of my petition is still there but immersed in and surrounded by God and it is God who now, in his very self, has my attention. The prayer of petition ends in the prayer of contemplation, where we no longer ask or talk but simply listen for God and let him do the asking.

Even if God knows my heart before I speak it, prayer, the prayer of asking, is still worthwhile. But *does* God know my heart before I speak it? Leaving aside the absurdity of speaking of before and after where the timeless God is concerned, we must say that certainly he knows the heart's powers, the direction it can and should take, he knows its weaknesses and strengths. But I don't think he knows what I want before I *say* what I want, precisely because until I say it, before I put my desire into words, it is simply not there. Words are important, not just as expressions of thoughts and desires, but as makers of them. So one may be friends with another, enjoy her company, feel lovingly toward her, but it's only when he says (in her presence or simply in imagination) "I love you" that desire for her becomes real and rooted. Indeed, the desire may be born in that very act of speech, and it's the words that give it birth.

I should rather think that both God and I know my prayer at the same time and *together* we form it, he, as always, taking the initiative, but relying on me to respond and with him bring the prayer to completion. Prayer is a dialogue between God and me in a deeper sense than we ordinarily think. It's not just God and me talking over my wants. It's more fundamentally God and me discovering my wants, and, more fundamentally still, making them.

So, for instance, I ask God for something. He replies: "Do you really want that?" I think it over and say: "Yes, I do." He says: "Prove it, both to me and to yourself." I think things over again, do some research, view the matter in God's presence, come back and say: "Yes, I really want it." He answers: "All right, then, let's see what *we* can do about it." And all the while he's there, touching, prodding my heart, speaking to me in and through his scriptures and saints and the whole of his creation. Little, if any of this, do I feel, of course, but I more deeply feel that this is the way it is, or might be if I took my prayer seriously.

Or it might be that I don't know what I want, or think that I should leave the whole thing up to God. And so I say to God: "What is it you want?" And he replies: "What is it that *you* want?" I say to him: "Thy will be done." He answers: "*Thy* will be done." Of course, God wants us to do his will, for therein lies our happiness, but his will is not independent of ours, and if we are to come into his kingdom we are to come with eyes open and of our own choosing. It's got to be *our* will as well as his.

The prime example of all of this is Jesus, throughout the whole of his lifetime but especially in his final days. At the Last Supper he prayed for his disciples and all the world. As he prayed he would now and again forget them, seemingly, and become lost in contemplation of the Trinity, the fullness of God. In the garden, in his agony, he spoke his will, what *he* wanted — "Let this chalice pass" — but he was even more concerned that his will be God's — "Nevertheless, not my will, but yours be done." The two wills finally merged into one, *both* Father and Son shaping the future. On the cross, again he prayed for us: "Father, forgive them . . ." but then became lost in the deepest contemplation, emptied of all, including God, to be filled *only* by God: "My God, my God, why have you forsaken me? . . . Father, into your hands I commend my spirit." When we ask Jesus, then, to teach us to pray it's this kind of praying that we should have in mind and at heart.

THREE

God and World

Many problems are solved, but many more arise, once the heart tells us that God — the God of Abraham, Isaac, and Jacob, the God of Jesus Christ — exists. For instance, there's the problem of creation. Since the Scopes trial till now how we've wrestled with it! Why did God create, how did he create, *did* he create? How bring mind and heart together in a wood as dark as this?

But is it, after all, so grave a problem? I read the first chapter of Genesis and I'm amazed by it. How in so few words could such powerful beauty and momentous truth be so harmoniously wedded? It's the worthy overture to the whole of the biblical narrative: it could have been "written" only by God. All the chief themes and truths of the Bible are there, at least in seed: the one God who is the maker of all, not, as in other ancient accounts of creation, through violent conflict with other gods, but by the simple gentle utterance of his word; the dignity of humankind, man and woman at the summit of creation, and creation's keepers and developers, not its possessors and exploiters; the goodness of all as it issues from a beneficent God; and the need to rest and let rest — worship God as above his creation as well as within it.

The Genesis overture is so beautifully narrated: simple words, simple images, almost a child's story. Imagine it as a Disney film. A screen of utter darkness at the opening with some suggestion of movement within it, and turbulent, chaotic sound bursting from it. Then a quiet, gentle but powerful voice: "Let there be light." Then gradually light out of darkness and harmony out of discord until the chaotic waters that fill the screen sparkle like diamonds . . . and on and on with all the color and sound and dignity inherent in the text itself until the making of humankind — man and woman at the word of God suddenly (or in slow, indistinct stages) appearing, one from the other, or with the other right from the start. Finally a sweeping, panoramic view of the whole and a subliminal suggestion of God within and beyond it.

What more do I expect of the text? The power of its truth and beauty prepares me for all the blend of story and history to come and helps me see more deeply into it. Need I ask, then, precisely *how* things got started? It all might have begun with a big bang — a sudden burst of energy as God's first biblical words might suggest — or in a more subdued manner, the cosmos slipping gently, quietly into being as life does now. God might only have made the seeds of things in the beginning — as St. Augustine conjectured — which then under his providence developed through the millenia. Things may have begun as things, more or less full grown and static at core, or on the run, as it were, in the very process of evolving. Biblical creation seems to me quite compatible with any of this as long as those fundamental truths that are its concern are respected. So, for the first human being(s) — full grown like the pagan Athena out of the head of Zeus, as the first chapter of Genesis suggests? Or did God, as in the Bible's second creation narrative, gradually shape humanity out of something more earthy so that both the heaven and earth of his making might glory as one? Whatever you like, providing what is more basic to the text is respected, namely the dignity of the human person as image of God.

That first chapter of Genesis is a summary of, a prelude to, the whole of the Judeo-Christian faith, from the one creator God in the beginning to rest in him in the end, with everything in between as good and, as with humankind, very good. It is also the pattern for right living and the learning process that fosters it.

"In the beginning, God..." It's a moot question among kmowledgeable Christians of our time whether we should begin with God or with his creation, with the divine or the human. Obviously for the child and the young adult creation comes first: they must and do discover the world and their own humanity before discovering God. The mature adult also begins with creation and most often ends with it, whether in the classroom, the home, at work or at play.

But whatever the temporal sequence, the priority in time, may be, *in depth* it is God who is to be first and last. Thus even in the education of the child, creation isn't to be presented as opaque with nothing more within or beyond it. It's there to be seen but also, like Alice's looking glass, to be seen through to the other side, to what brings it into being, lives within it, loves and sustains it. This same pattern of learning is to be carried on into adult life with greater seriousness and energy, though also with the lightness and joy with which it began.

But if God is to be found in his creation he must even *temporally* be found prior to it. The instinct, the heart, the faith that strains toward him must at the very start of the educational process, even with the child, be acknowledged and nourished, through revelation heard, prayed over, and lived. Him whom we would find in his creation, as the depth of creation, we must first have met in our heart. "In the beginning, God."

"Let there be light." Not a manichaean or agnostic darkness, but light, the intelligibility of God and his creation. The critical, sceptical mind is essential: "Rarely affirm, seldom deny, always distinguish." All who have some sense of the immensity of God and his creation and the relative littleness of the human mind would agree, I think, with this medieval scholastic wisdom. Truth, especially that which has to do with God, is slippery business: Now we have it, now we don't. But a *radical* scepticism and agnosticism is to have no abiding place among those who worship the God who has suffused his creation with light, and is himself Light. Therefore he expects us to *see*. Not the whole picture, certainly, but enough to see our way by, step by step, and to glimpse him and his providence all along the way.

"Let there be. . ." Within the light, God creates. Sun, moon, stars above; seas, land, plants, animals. He creates everything. Whatever is in whatever way has his creative touch deep within it; it's good and good to know. So we have the arts and sciences, not simply to satisfy our curiosity and our native instinct to create, but out of love for him who made all things: care for me, care for the dear work of my hands — know it, love it, teach it, and help me make it the dearer.

Know it not piecemeal — this or that aspect of it in isolation — but the totality of it: the whole of the truth. We live in an age of analysis, where everything — including the human person — is broken down into bits and pieces: Humpty-dumpty shattered and lying all over the place with no one to put him back together again. The crying need today is not for further analysis but synthesis, trying once again to see God and his world whole. In a world of infinite complexity an impossible job, but to God and the faith he gives all things are possible.

"Let us make man. . ." At the pinnacle of creation is the making of humankind, requiring the fullness of God's power and love: not, as with the rest of creation, "Let there be. . .," but "Let *us* make. . ." Herein is revealed the dignity of the human being, and the human being as such without respect to nation, race, color, or, indeed, creed, for no such distinctions were there "in the beginning." There was but one physical world, diverse but unified and harmonized by the one creative touch of God, and one world of humankind. Both physical world and humankind have been analyzed and fragmented to death and cry out for healing and wholeness. We were made in the image and likeness of God that we might know that our job is not to break up and destroy but to mend and create, and to do this, as God does, not violently (the bloody revolution meant to set things right) but gently, by simple word and creative action: "Let there be light...Let us make man." And that "man" is man and woman: "Male and female he created *them*." But here too what God had originally joined we have put asunder. Again, the synthesizing mind and heart are needed, with a major portion of our education, accordingly, directed toward this end.

"On the seventh day God rested." In the space of a single breath, a few simple words, three times the sabbath is mentioned. There's a place for action: six days in which to work, to build up the world. But the contemplative is also essential: to let ourselves and the world lie fallow and not glut ourselves to the world's and our irreparable harm. This is why at the beginning of this grand overture, "the Spirit of God hovered over the waters" — the Spirit who is and gives the high gift of wisdom, loving knowledge, the simple beholding of contemplation. Out of this emerges the whole of creation and into it all is meant to return and rest. Yes, we begin and we end with God and the recognition that it's his world not ours. We are caretakers, cocreators, guardians of a world made for all God's children. We are to be educated, then, and are to educate in such action, the kind that has its beginning and end in the contemplative knowing and loving of God.

"And God said...and God said...and God said..." In the beginning was not so much action as a sermon. God doesn't do, he speaks the world. This should tell us something about words, the words used in our preaching and teaching, and it should tell us something of the nobility of preaching and teaching. A poet has said, "Where word leaves off, no thing may be." We think of words simply as the expression of thought or feeling. But they're much more than this. They also create thought and feeling, they inspire and direct action. They make the world and they break it. So this first song of the Bible would have us be careful of words, of language. It would have us listen carefully to them, use them sparingly and reverently, teach them wisely and lovingly to those who thirst for them in order to *live*. So much does God love words that with them, and them alone, he creates the world, and it's as Word that he becomes flesh and lives among us. Our own love and use of words ought to be something of a match for his.

One big question remains that this first chapter of Genesis doesn't quite answer, and that is *why* God created. At the time Genesis was sung/written, I suppose, it sufficed to know *that* he did. Further questioning might not have been well received, as poor old Job was to discover. But come that other later magnificent prelude deliberately echoing this one, the question is raised and answered. "In the beginning was the Word . . . and the Word was made flesh . . . filled with enduring love." The gospel of John together with the other gospels and every book of the New Testament proclaims that love is God's motive for *everything*. Not any kind of love, but that which is expansive, love that must grow and foster growth, that moves out of self and into the other. If God is such love then I can begin to see the why of creation. It's almost as though he had to create, just as when I'm filled with love I've got to sing and dance and shout for joy and embrace and *make* love and make babies or pictures or music or poems — all a faint shadow of the great love that first moved God to create and then moved him to embrace his creation and make it ever more true and beautiful. He *had* to create? Not quite, because being fundamentally love he's also freedom.

But under pressure of such great love how compelled that freedom must be to surrender itself! God may not have had to create, but he sure did want to!

Also to be considered is the problem of a changeless Creator-God in a world of change — not as a nut in a shell or the fruit in its skin, but as vitally, organically one with it. The visible, tangible, audible human Jesus does not just hold and envelop God. He *is* God. When he walks, talks, joys, suffers, dies, changes in any way, it is God who is acting, suffering, changing. Jesus tells us, among other things, that God is of a piece with the whole of creation, at the heart of every change, involved in every change, yet himself remaining still and absolutely changeless. "All that is good, all that is perfect, is given us from above; it comes down from the Father of all light; with him there is no such thing as alteration, no shadow caused by change" (Jas 1:17). In faith, let me try to understand . . .

Everything changes. People in the know tell me this, and I believe it. Change is *the* concept of our time, one of the most prominent words in our vocabulary. There's the changing fetus in the mother's womb, the dramatic change from womb to birth, and all the changes, minute and mammoth, from then until death, the most awesome change of all. There are the changes in customs, morality, and politics from one generation to another; changes in the clothes we wear, what we eat and drink, what we live in, drive in, what we suffer and die in. The great stars, once thought to be so constant, we know now to be constantly on the move and forever altering within, bursting, and being formed anew. The smallest atom and particle within the atom move so fast that no one of them can be captured and focused by our almost equally fast moving machines; they can only be observed fleetingly and en masse. The very table before me, which seems so firm and solid, is, as the physicists tell me (and I believe them), a wild whirligig of atoms. So also for the great massive mountains — the "eternal hills" of the Bible — the ocean, rivers, and lakes, all in wondrous perpetual motion. Heraclitus of ancient Greece had said it as well as any of our modern sophisticates: "You can't put your finger into the same stream twice." His precocious student, Cratylus, corrected him and said it even better: "You can't put your finger into the same stream once," so fast does it move and your finger change.

But equally with change I'm aware of the constant, not as separate from change but within it and one with it. Change itself, paradoxically, is a constant: It's *always* there in everything. Customs change but there are always customs. Morality and politics change but there's always some form of morality, some form of politics even if it's anarchy. We wear different things at different times but always we wear something to protect us from sun and storm, if only an extra layer of skin, more or less hair or fur, or some trinket or paint to adorn the body. Though always on the move internally and externally, the stars are still the stars, the atom is always the atom, and the mountains, oceans, rivers, lakes, no matter how prodigious their movements, remain what they always were. I myself have undergone so many changes from before birth till now, yet beneath and one with it all, abiding every change, are my unique genes and bloodcells, fingerprints, voice patterns and basic psychological and spiritual orientation. My DNA — the god of modern science — is undeniably constant, they tell me, one and the same from here unto eternity. Love too is a marvelous constant. Though we love in different and changing ways according to changing time, place, circumstance, we still always love and make love, or at least yearn to do so.

If we remain only on the surface — of our mind and of things — then, yes, there will be for us only change. But if we get *within* the change and deep within our mind then the constant becomes just as obvious, like the ocean churning and heaving in a storm — on the surface it's all change, chaotic wildness and fury, but as we plunge beneath its surface and enter its depths we find a stillness that becomes more and more profound the deeper we go. We find that our own lives and all the change within them have most meaning when we can escape from or transcend or delve deeply within them to a place of calm. And so we're forever searching, at least in fantasy, for some quiet meadow or mountaintop or temple or love — some eye within the hurricane — where all movement and change cease and we and all else are at last still and at peace.

You, my God, are this eye within the storm, this quiet meadow and mountaintop, this holy temple and deep, deep love. Not that you are static and lifeless, but that you're alive and active beyond calculation. Not that you're without movement and change, but that these are so perfect within you that they are absolutely one with your eternal constancy. Your greatest theologian was wont to describe you as "Pure Act" — so much alive that you're absolutely but dynamically still. When the light bulb above my desk is weak and defective I can see the movement of its light: It flickers and flutters, grows dim, and finally dies. But when it's perfect it's so actively moving that it's constant, wondrously still and bright. Or when I'm in deepest thought or love, all around and within me is silent and at rest, and time, the measure of movement, seems suspended. Constancy and change — not opposed to each other but rather, together in some ineffable oneness at the heart of a reality that reflects, as it flows from, the fullness of life that is constantly and eternally you, my God.

The world is alive with the Spirit of God. For a long time we thought of the world as a great machine, each part functioning closely amd delicately with the other, like the wheels and springs of a fine watch, like the hardware and software

of a computer. The human being was considered a minia-
ture machine within the larger one, equipped with computer
brain, plastic heart, synthetic bone and muscle, and an elec-
trical network that kept the whole thing buzzing. All was a
bit more complex and much less ugly than the monster created by Dr. Frankenstein, but basically the idea was the same.
We were all of us sophisticated robots, sometimes touching
one another and interacting, again like parts of a watch, but
radically and forever distinct, never merging, never becoming vitally and organically one. And once we understood each
of the parts we could anticipate the functioning of the whole
from now to the last syllable of time. All was neat, clean, tidy,
and predictable under the sway of Unalterable Law.

Such was the world of Newtonian physics. Then Einstein
came along and changed all that. Now the universe began
to look more like a process than a thing, more like a living
organism than a mechanical toy, and it became far less predictable. James Jeans spoke of it as a giant thought; Werner
Heisenberg introduced into our speculations the principle of
uncertainty; and Einstein and his disciples convinced us that
the observer enters into the observed and thereby changes it,
that matter is energy and energy matter, and that everything
is relative to everything else because each is *within* the other.

Things are seen now not discretely but in living context:
They move into each other, merge with each other. Each is
still distinct — I am not you and you are not me, and neither
of us is stone or plant or dog. Yet where precisely does the one
leave off and the other begin? My neck, my shoulder, arm, and
hand, my brain, heart, veins and arteries — severed one from
the other and arranged neatly upon the dissecting table you
can point to each separately. But as organic parts of the living
whole that is me, each *is* the other. That underlying energy
we call life not only unites them in a functioning whole but
merges them one into the other: My neck is *in* my shoulder,
my shoulder in my arm, my heart is in my brain and my brain

in my heart. There are levels of this energy and somewhere within them even the stone, the dog, the plant and I, and God himself, merge and blend. Each is different toward the surface, but down deep the same vital force and driving energy permeates all, makes us one and, as one, drives us forward. It is a power unknown and unpredictable because at heart it is the purest freedom.

This *living* world in all its unified complexity once again begins to engage our interest. I say "once again" because once upon a time it was humankind's only kind of world. In the religions of the east it was (and is) the one transcendent all-pervasive life and energy which is the very life of all and which alone is real; all the rest is *maya*, illusion. Old Parmenides in ancient Greece and the remarkably infectious Plotinus were of similar mind: Illusion is in the many, reality in the absolute and undivided One. Jesus, too, while respecting and loving each distinct, unique human being, would have us look to our common, living root: "I am the vine,/ you are the branches./ Whoever remains in me, with me in him,/ bears fruit in plenty;/ for cut off from me you can do nothing" (Jn 15:5). And he prays, "May they all be one,/ just as, Father, you are in me and I am in you,/ so that they also may be in us" (Jn 17:21). St. Paul picked up on this *in*dwelling of Father, Son, and Spirit within themselves and us. We are not just one with God but are in God. With the Greeks Paul is comfortable in speaking of the God "*in* whom we live and move and have our being" (Acts 17:28, *NAB*). But he's much more emphatic than they. Taught by the Master, he revels in telling us we are in Christ and Christ in us. We are not just near to Christ, we are of his very body, each of us as organs vitally dependent on each other, and all of us dependent upon the energy and love of Christ our head. He writes of the Spirit not as something outside us but as our very life and love, who prays within us and who groans within all creation toward the "glorious freedom of the children of God" (Rom 8:21).

Many today are groping to rediscover this vision of the world. It has been long lost, even within the Christian churches. God has been someone "out there" with little enough to do with the world — the great clock winder who first set things on their course and then withdrew into isolated splendor. Christ became an external "moral force" inspiring us to good deeds, or if within, still apart from *us*, like the fruit within the rind. God's grace was an accumulation of giftwrapped packages we stored within us and periodically opened to be assured of God's favor toward us. And our relationships with each other had to be in and through the body with no other possibilities of loving intercourse.

All along the way, from Jesus till now, there have been men and women — saints and mystics we call them — who thought and lived otherwise, but they were relatively rare. Now, however, vast numbers are beginning to take uncertain steps toward what they consider something new. The mysticism of the new science alone would have only esoteric appeal. But philosophers, theologians, poets, and the popular press have given it a more universal language. I think of Teilhard de Chardin — more scientist, perhaps, than philosopher, more poet than theologian, yet enough of all four to inspire much of our contemporary world to take a second look and consider the possibilities: deep, vital Spirit alive in and through all; intercommunication on the level of spirit as well as body; grace as an energy and a love that we *are* rather than have; Christ as the very life and love of the universe, his mystical body being not mere metaphor but the most potent of realities. I think also of the popularization of eastern religions in the west, the serious acceptance and investigation and development of paranormal powers and phenomena (ESP and all the rest), a plethora of books and workshops on meditation and contemplative prayer, communes of love and empathetic living, and active environmental concern as a spirituality of the earth.

I'm not saying that we now have saints and mystics running around all over the place. Far from it. What we have, for the most part, are dabblers, dilettantes of the spirit, those who get their kicks out of religion as others out of drugs. But even these have begun to see and long for, if only feebly, the world as life and not machine, God within and not just without, a universal interconnectedness that is at least a shadow of the substance of Christ's mystical body. It's a beginning. As a matter of fact it sounds much like the beginnings Paul found among the gentiles as he preached their own Unknown God *in* whom was all being, life, and movement (Acts 17:16–34). What immediate effect Paul had in trying to deepen that gentile belief who knows; but the long-range results have been impressive, to say the least. Like him we can only begin at the beginning, work with it, and hope and pray for the best.

The problem of pain is, for many, the greatest there is when an infinitely good, infinitely powerful creator is postulated. In Albert Camus' novel/parable *The Plague*, doctor and priest confront each other over suffering, especially that of the innocent. Both agree that suffering is incomprehensible. The priest suggests that perhaps we should love what we can't understand. The atheist doctor unhesitatingly and angrily replies: "Until my dying day I shall refuse to love a scheme of things in which children are put to torture."

To love suffering, as the priest suggests, is a dangerous proposal to say the very least. Images of sadism and masochism arise, deviations terrible when unleashed and run wild. Images of indifference also surface: There stand the sick and the dying, the hungry, the lonely, the abandoned, while I sit comfortably here with full stomach and quiet mind lovingly writing about it all. Love my own suffering, maybe, but the suffering of others? Here I'm one mind with the doctor,

as with Christ himself: Give it no quarter, especially when it
is of the innocent.

But hatred for the whole scheme of things? Hardly. My
innate faith responds positively to the Catholic Christian creed
that the world, especially in the overall scheme of things,
is fundamentally good, though seriously marred; otherwise I
think that long ago I would with little if any regret have blown
my unhappy head off. What keeps me alive and fairly happy
to be alive is the knowledge, whether of mind or heart, of
rooted loveliness.

> There lives the dearest freshness deep down things;
> And though the last lights off the black West went
> Oh, morning, at the brown brink eastward, springs —
> Because the Holy Ghost over the bent
> World broods with warm breast and with ah! bright
>   wings.

Yes, there's evil in the world, often tragic, sometimes
of diabolic magnitude. But the good outside me and within
bears witness that evil does not have the final word. However grave it might be, there's that in the human being that
continually struggles against it and strives for a better world.
There are exceptions. People do give up, sometimes termi-
nally. And death is all about us. But wonder of wonders,
most by far continue to live and want to live and believe
they should always live. Isn't this evidence that the "scheme
of things" is right; that there is "the dearest freshness deep
down things"? Often we have to search for it and continually mend what is wrong, but the fact is that we do search
and we do mend and we do not give up, at least for long. In
spite of evil something outside us and within keeps us hoping
even beyond hope. This must be because something within
us keeps seeing beyond sight into the goodness of God and
his world.

Still, I'm troubled by evil, especially as it infects and destroys the innocent. If the world issues from the hands of a loving, compassionate God whence comes the evil? Not from God, surely, at least as my inmost faith responds to him. A God of Yin and Yang, of Light and Dark, a manichaean divinity of good and evil, spirit and matter might offer some a way out of the difficulty. I'm not looking for a way out, though, but a way in. And once in God I can find only love, goodness, and light.

It seems to me the origin of evil is closer to hand. "Jesus knew all people and did not trust himself to them; he never needed evidence about anyone; he could tell what someone had in him" (Jn 2:24–25). If of an evening I drink too much and suffer a hangover the next morning it would be silly of me to blame God. Evidently, I myself am to blame. If one given to sexual promiscuity or mainlining contracts AIDS I don't say: "See God's punishment upon him." The punishment is self-inflicted, the sickness and death *naturally* follow from an abuse of nature, as air, water, and earth pollution result not from divine vindictiveness but from human greed and carelessness and indifference. The sickness and death of that child born syphilitic is not God's fault. Someone else along the way abused love, and so destroyed the innocent. The world may one day be wracked and ruined by yet another holocaust, racial or nuclear. God's doing? No more than the holocausts of the past. Why not put the blame for evil where it belongs — upon the men and women who live and act outside a God who made all things well and would have us do likewise.

But this compassionate God is all-powerful, isn't he? Why, then, doesn't he do something about the evil — prevent it, cure it, make it go away? Depends on what you mean by "power." Powerful to create? Yes. Powerful to destroy? Maybe. I suppose if he wished, God could undo all that he has made, including humankind and the freedom at its core

— if he wished. The qualification makes all the difference. All his power springs from the deepest roots of power which are of truth and love; these are for creation and growth and in no way for violation and destruction. At least this is the way of God as revealed in Jesus Christ. Maybe God is powerless — in our understanding of the word — in the face of evil, as Jesus in fact was: All evil was heaped upon him in the space of a few hours and he, God, could only suffer it. Both love and truth seem to require such apparent passivity of him — truth, because God has made us free to make or unmake the world and so in truth must respect our freedom, even when we use it to destroy, or else stand as liar and cheat. Love requires the same, for love to be love must be grounded in freedom: I must be free to love and free to accept love. Thus Jesus doesn't pressure or cajole, doesn't try to force a loving response. "'Rabbi, where do you live?' . . . 'Come and see'" (Jn 1:38–39). In order to make quite clear that he would not force but only elicit love he said what he later proved in fact: "When I am lifted up from the earth, I shall *draw* all people to myself" (Jn 12:32).

This is not to say that God does nothing in the face of evil. In historic fact he did what perennial myth dreamed he might: He became incarnate that he might do battle with evil. But again, the battle wasn't of our kind: force against force with destruction all over the place. The weapons of God were truth and love, which together make that word that "cuts more incisively than any two-edged sword" (Heb 4:12). What God does do is help us, if we wish, to clean up the mess we ourselves make. I harm myself and others, and God, who respects my freedom to do so, lets it be done. But he stands close to me still, waiting, like the prodigal's father, for me to come back to him that he might, with me, make things well again. He cannot destroy with me but we can together create anew. Further, he's there at the very start, before we begin our use or abuse of freedom. He's outside us in his revelation, the gospel story of his life which is the pattern and inspiration for the right use of freedom. His saints, his holy ones past and present, particularize his pattern and inspiration so that we can read Jesus in events and circumstances closer to our own lives. And God is *within* us, that "still, small voice" of his whispering his will to us and prompting our freedom to move in creative ways.

For the innocent and for those who suffer and die in innocence, there is the *vita nuova*, the new life Jesus, *the* innocent one, gained for us. I can destroy the innocent, I can abuse and slay children, and God, however sadly for him and for us, must respect my liberty to do so. But once I've had my way then he can begin again to have his. So after I have slain Jesus, hurled him into the night of death, he rises from the dead into new, transcendent life, not alone but with all the innocent of every place and time. So my Christian faith teaches, and, once again, my own inner faith, which always reaches beyond this world, responds. Heaven is not a fiction of my mind; it is the reality of my heart.

The statement that God is not the cause of evil requires qualification. In a sense he may be thought of as causing the particular evil of pain and suffering. Initially such evil, as every other kind of evil, derives from a human misuse of freedom. But once it's there pain and suffering are required in order to remove it. If, for instance, through my own fault or that of others I become addicted to drugs or alcohol, I eventually suffer terrible mental and physical suffering and cause the same in others. But if I attend to the word of God outside and within me and want to change, I must now suffer the pain of withdrawal and of the required reorientation of my life. This, however, is the pain not of destruction and disintegration but of growth, and as such may be the offspring of God's loving action upon me.

It's as though I were digging a pit and with every passing day moving deeper and deeper into it. As the darkness blackens and the air grows thin and the space narrows I become claustrophobic and long for the upper reaches of light and space and air. But the ascent's too steep and I'm much too feeble for it. Wearily I look up to the distant light and there I see one with rope in hand asking if he might help me. I answer yes, and immediately the rope is in my hand. I begin to mount but the going is painful. My lungs are bad, my arms and legs weak. Several times I want to let go but my friend above pleads with me to hold on for a while longer; I tell him it's too difficult. I might cry out against him, might curse him for not having let me be, might even blame him for all my woe. The bottom of the pit was bad but the climb out is even worse! He keeps insisting, keeps the rope steady and secure, and promises that soon, after all the agony and pain, I will once again know the space and freedom I had lost.

In this sense I may wish, even long for suffering, for myself and others, and rejoice when it's upon me. *Aut pati aut mori*, cries the saint: "Let me suffer or let me die." This may be judged masochistic only by those who don't sense how far they are from God and how close they're meant to be. We might compare it to the agony and anguish, the physical and mental pain involved in sheer-rock climbing. For true mountaineers, those who would get to the top at whatever cost, even the pain, *especially* the pain, becomes a joy.

But is it altogether true that the human being and not God is the first cause of evil? What of earthquakes, tornadoes, hurricanes, conflagrations? All were there, say the geologists, long before humanity came on the scene, were there to greet it when at last it arrived. What of the quite natural process of growing old and dying and all the suffering therein involved for the victim and even more, sometimes, for the bereaved? What of blind nature's tooth and claw that bite into the human being without the mediation of human freedom? Quite obviously, not everything that issued from the hand of God was in fact good.

So says my mind. Or does it? As rooted in my faith it manages another perspective. Earthquakes, tornadoes, and other natural disasters are not in themselves evils. In fact, if we could be secure on some outside planet and watch mother earth behave at her "worst," violently and all at once erupting, flooding, bursting into volcanic flame we would rather find it all quite fascinating and beautiful, much as we do the sun when we observe through our scopes its mad and capricious dance of fire, or when we see a volcano from a secure distance. When humankind happened, again say the geologists, things were relatively peaceful here below. Might not there have been, then, some garden of Eden, some place of innocence where a kindly God kept his prize creature from serious mishap? Where the first human beings, like a later St. Francis, lived in harmony and peace with nature, gave nature her due and received the same from her?

These first human beings need not have been super humans with the brain capacity of their modern offspring. They need not have been Einsteins and Madame Curies, nor have had the kind of physical beauty that our particular time and place prizes. But they may well have been far ahead in moral truth and beauty, much as some innocent children I have known and been quietly in awe of, and may have had the farseeing wisdom and sensitivity to the beautiful that innocence seems to manage.

What, then, went wrong? I don't know. Freedom was there, and where freedom is anything can happen. But evidently something did go wrong, and then hostility began to build between man and woman, man and man, woman and woman, humans and animals and all of nature, much as it does now through lust, greed, violence, pride, envy, and, worst of all, perhaps, sloth and neglect. The first fall is always the greatest. Not that evil sprang up full grown; but somewhere in the distant past the seed was planted and it would grow and bear its fruit. What once was could never again be, unless. . . .

True to himself and his creature God must permit evil to be. Otherwise freedom becomes a fiction and a farce. But, as ancient faith proclaimed, his wisdom and love continually bring good out of evil, such that the last state of affairs can become even better than the first. "O happy fault, O blessed night!" is our Easter cry as we look back upon that first sin in light of the Resurrection about to be celebrated. *God's* freedom now becomes even more intensely operative in a frenzy of grace. God himself becomes flesh to show us the way, thus healing our blindness; in eucharistic love he enters anew within us to prompt us along the way. Through an alertness inspired by the Spirit we now become less liable to sloth and neglect. Greed and lust and violence pale before the generosity, deep love, and gentleness of our Savior. Pride and envy are diminished as we are moved to live God's own humility and his joy in the good of others. In God's Spirit, breathed into us by Christ, we try through science, medicine, engineering, art, education, prayer, works of justice and charity — the whole spectrum of mind and heart — to put the world back together again. At least the ideal and real possibility for re-creation is there and sometimes the fact of it surfaces in awesome splendor.

Suffering itself acquires unexpected value: The Apostle declares, "It makes me happy to be suffering for you now, and in my own body to make up all the hardships that still have to be undergone by Christ for the sake of his body, the Church" (Col 1:24). We think of creativity only in terms of action: We build the world by what we do. But Christ's life teaches that passion is even more effective than action: Through his suffering and death on the cross, more than by anything he said or did, Christ redeemed the world. And it's mainly through the suffering and death of his servants that he continues to redeem it.

Such vicarious suffering is a scandal and foolishness to those with no experience of faith. Yet, after two thousand years, the cross remains the center of Christian belief. Enter a Catholic church and the cross, the crucifix, is everywhere. We wear it around our necks, it begins and ends our rosaries, we sign ourselves with it before and after prayer. And at the absolute center of our principal act of Christian worship is the reminder and re-enactment not of the deeds of Christ but of his suffering and death: "This is my body which will be given up for you... This is the cup of my blood which will be shed for you. Do *this* in memory of me."

This is why when all is said and done Christianity offers no answer to the problem of pain. It might do as I have tried to do: set our minds at partial rest by making as best use of our heads as we can. But in the end it simply points to the crucifix. "Why have they done this to me?" cries the tortured, wracked, and dismembered victim of a terrible injustice. From the crucifix in his cell a voice echoes: "Why have they done this to *me*?" So the medieval tale has it.

Only a pious story? Once when visiting my dying father in hospital I stopped to visit a woman whose room I had often passed and simply smiled my greeting. The nurse had told me the woman had been bedridden for years, paralyzed from her waist down. I was amazed to find her joyful and outgoing, with little if any concern about herself. After some conversation I had to ask her how she managed to be so cheerful. She simply glanced at the small crucifix hanging from the exercise bar above her and said: "You should know, Father." I didn't, but through her I was on my way to learning.

Years later while on a brief retreat at the leper colony in Kalaupapa, Hawaii, the sister nurse took me to the bed of the colony's oldest inhabitant: Father Damien was still alive when she came as a little girl. She was blind, half her face was gone, and she had stumps for arms. Quietly, reverently the sister said, "Mary, Father is here to see you." For the tears in my throat I could say nothing as I saw her face glow and her right arm feebly move toward head, breast, shoulders. . . . Ultimately, the only answer to the problem of pain seems to be the cross. But it's an answer that takes more than the head to appreciate. It demands one's whole person and Christ himself hanging on the cross *within* us.

The fundamental problem out of which all the others arise: our failure to appreciate the magnitude of God and his love and our freedom to respond to it. We make God too small and our liberty insignificant.

FOUR

Christianity

There have been and are so many different religions. I think of the ancient religions of Greece and Persia and of the Germanic and Celtic peoples, of the North and South American Indians. There are the great abiding religions of the Far East and Middle East: Hinduism, Buddhism, Judaism, Islam. There are the many different religions of the African peoples, the various cults and sects that continually spring up like wild flowers in every part of the world. There are those who have or claim to have a religion private unto themselves. Then there's Christianity, and within Christianity churches that sometimes appear to be their own distinct religion, having little if anything to do with the Christianity of history.

Amid this potpourri I ask why I am a Christian, specifically a Catholic Christian. I can only answer this question from the point of view of one particular Catholic Christian. A subjective approach to be sure, but how else deal with such a matter as intimate as one's religion? Besides, the subjective may hold a fair share of objective truth, depending upon who's the subject, I suppose, and what is said and how it's said. Let me try for an answer.

First, I'm a Christian because it's been given to me to be such: "Simon son of Jonah you are a blessed man! Because it was no human agency that revealed this to you but my Father in heaven." Thus said Jesus in the gospel of Matthew. The very beginning of John's gospel proclaims that those who

71

believe in Jesus' name are those "who were born not from human stock or human desire or human will but from God himself" (Jn 1:13). That one is made Christian by God's grace is written across almost every page of St. Paul and across the many centuries of Christianity to the present day.

Granted, had I been born of Hindu, or Buddhist, or Moslem parents I would today most likely be of their faith. But that I was in fact born and raised a Christian I take to be a particular grace, a gift of God drawing me into the fullness of his revelation. And since I'm not a determinist I believe I have been free all along the way to change my religion as many another has done. Indeed, several times in my life I've been severely tempted to give up on God altogether; but something has kept me faithful, more or less. If in the beginning my faith was passed on to me without my asking, at a later date in full maturity I was interiorly converted to it such that now I was Christian because I freely and fully chose to be. And so I have been, am, and hope to remain a Christian.

How, then, do I look upon all these other religions vis-a-vis my own? Excepting those which have been and are *in very principle* destructive or constrictive of the human being and condition, I regard them, especially the great world religions, as preparation, past and present, for the acceptance of Christ. Thus the religion of Moses and the prophets, as well as the great poetry, philosophy, and religion of the Greeks and Romans, prepared for the coming of Christ. Religions of today may serve the same purpose. But I also see them as part of the fullness of Christianity. I as an individual know something of Christ; the professed Christian world as a whole, past and present, knows much more. But all is so little compared to all that can be known. And if Jesus is present to me and my little world why not to the rest of the world and in ways that might appear foreign to me? "It is the Lord," said the beloved disciple some time *after* he and the others had failed to recognize him (Jn 21:7). I may, then, learn (and

have learned) something of Christ from religions other than
my own.

Other religions offer the world a doctrine, a way of life
(Tao), they proclaim and inspire the search for wisdom (Zen).
So their holy ones are the gurus, the teachers, of the way,
the wisdom. Christianity has a doctrine too — from the Commandments of the Old Law to the Sermon on the Mount to
Jesus' farewell words at the Last Supper, but it offers much
more than this. It offers God himself — God not so much
above us and out of reach — unless through long, hard as-
cetical practice — but come down to us, becoming one of
us, living and dying and rising for love of us, and wanting
our love in return. My God is personal, and intimately so.
In the total context of the gospel, when Jesus says, "I am
the way . . ." the emphasis is not on "the way," as with the
Taoist, but the "I." Jesus himself is his teaching: "Come, follow *me* . . . Take up your cross and follow *me* . . . Learn of *me*
for I am meek and humble of heart. . . *I* am the vine and you
are the branches. . . *I* am the light of the world." At the Last
Supper as recorded by John, Jesus teaches sublime doctrine,
the highest of mystical truth, but the high point of that meal
was the meal itself transformed into his very self: "Take and
eat, this is my body. . . Take and drink, this is the cup of my
blood." Jesus himself, more than his wisdom, is "the Bread
of Life."

Thus the Christian holy one isn't so much the wise one as
the lover, and, if wise, only because she first learned to love,
as Thérèse of Lisieux, who was no great shakes as an as-
cetic, no specialist in lofty wisdom, but was all love, "foolish
love" of another *person*: "*aimer Jesus a la folie . . . ma vocation, c'est l'amour.*" Or as Catherine of Siena who revelled
not so much in her love for God as in God's mad, drunken
love for her — He was "*pazzo d'amore . . . ebro d'amore*"
for her who of herself was nothing. What a gift *this* revelation would be to other religions, which have not as yet

realized it. What a gift it would be to me if only *I* might realize it!

This Person, this God of Christianity, is both human and divine: not simply the appearance of the divine in the human, but the human in very truth become divine, while still remaining itself. My instinct, then, that religion to be true must worship a God who is both transcendent and immanent is proved right. Because God became flesh all flesh and all that's touched by it becomes not just good now, but holy: mind, heart, imagination, memory, senses, body from head to toe. Because God in his flesh stepped into the river Jordan all the waters of the world became holy. Because he looked up into the sky all of space became holy. Because he touched the flowers and contemplated the birds of the air all life became holy. For Christians, then, the fundamental attitude before the world and one another is not just respect but reverence, and all violation of the world is sacrilege.

But because it was *God* who became flesh we must now look deep within and beyond the world. "To love another is to worship the divine in her." Reverence, and more than this, hope — for what is above and beyond. We are to love and worship flesh and world, but however beautiful and holy they are, ultimately they must fail us. They can become twisted and ugly, can turn upon and strike me even unto death. The whole world can blow up in my face and leave me isolated and terribly alone. Still I'm not alone, there's yet someone to love and be loved by because God, the best of all, survives all loss. The great living symbol of this is the incarnate God himself. So beautiful the flesh of Jesus in all his words and deeds, yet so ugly and disappointing there on the cross: the grand failure. But within and beyond the wracked body of the man abides the Spirit of God. When all else, including the human Jesus, fails and fades, God remains to draw us to himself alone, and then, in his own good time and manner, to raise up, restore, and renew what was lost.

This it is that makes me a missionary. I have the gift of my Christian faith from the Lord. This gift is so profoundly beautiful that I must spend my life searching it and want others to join me in the quest. But I don't want to force it upon them. Jesus himself used no such force, only invitation: "Come and see." And so I want to invite others to look Jesus over. I want them to see Jesus as I do, but more, to see him in their own lives, their own culture, their own religion. "The kingdom of God is at hand. . . The kingdom of God is within *you.*" Maybe between what I have to say to them and they to me we might both see God more fully and serve him better.

Christianity is above all a matter of love. Not a vague, abstract love that functions at a distance, but one that's up close, intimate, concrete. It's love of the individual. Other systems of belief recognize divinity as something impersonal: a first cause or prime mover that sets things going and then is heard of no more (Aristotle, deists and some present day science), or as a final cause that attracts love but doesn't give it (Plato, Lucretius, and contemporary religious aesthetes), or as the interior prompter of our own love for the beloved (reflective lovers of every generation). But in Christ we find a God who *in addition* to creating the universe out of love, preserving it in love, and prompting and attracting love, does himself love each and every one of us, and with a *passion.* "No one can have greater love than to lay down one's life for one's friends." Christ — God — did this, and for each one of us, for we are his friends: "I call you friends, because I have made known to you everything I have learned from my Father" (Jn 15:13–15).

On every page of the gospel I read this manifestation of God's individual love. At the beginning of the great history we find God not looking to put a vote to the masses as to whether he should be born among us, but rather appealing to a single person: He loves a solitary woman with such intense love that she says yes, and so begins the Incarnation. At Cana the plight of a single couple and the request of one individual elicits the first of Jesus' "signs." When Jesus chooses his disciples he doesn't gather a crowd and ask for volunteers but calls and selects each individually. He has special friends — Martha, Mary, Lazarus, Mary Magdalene, Peter, Andrew, Nathanael, James, Philip, the Beloved Disciple. He heals with an individual touch. Out of all those crowding and jostling him he recognizes the hand of a woman on his garment, loves her for it, and heals her of her sickness. He often draws his "patients" aside from the crowd to be alone with them as he heals them. Once, it's said, he even took the individual outside the town to work the cure. He describes the good shepherd as one who leaves the ninety-nine and goes off in search of the one who's lost. Indeed, he seems to have a distaste for crowds, always trying to escape them, going off to the desert or mountain alone or with a few intimates. He's contentedly alone with the Samaritan woman and with the adulteress (whose part he takes against "the crowd") and with Nicodemus. At the end, when he knew it was the end, he didn't — as we might expect and as others have done — summon a crowd and make a final statement before the world. Instead he invited a few close friends for a quiet, intimate meal, touching and speaking with each of them. Even in his passion, though the crowd is there, the gospels emphasize Christ and the individual: Pilate, Mary, John, a few faithful women, the good thief. And in his resurrection, again, contrary to what we might expect — Jesus manifesting himself to the whole world as victorious — he appears to only a few, and again with the greatest intimacy: "Mary . . . Rabboni" (Jn 20:16), "Simon son of John, do you love me?" (Jn 21:16).

The wonder of this should be ample food for our meditations: God's great and intimate love for *me* as an individual. Out of all the billions of people who are and have been, still he loves *me*. But as wonderful as such a revelation is I can't stop there. I must move on from God's love to mine. Since I am in the image of God I must imitate his kind of love and so love the individual. "Love one another, *as* I have loved you" (Jn 15:12).

The church early learned this lesson. Its love was for the isolated individual: the scattered poor, lowly, and insignificant — not so much those at the organized, prestigious center but alone and outcast on the fringes of society. It began hospices and hospitals for the quite dispensable sick and dying, orphanages for helpless, abandoned children so much in need of an individual love, schools and eventually universities, which originally were not for the great and powerful but for the poor in body that they might at least have some richness of mind. Later the state saw that the church had a good thing going and so started its own hospitals, orphanages, schools and universities. Then began bigness, numbers, forms to fill out, efficiency at the expense of the personal. The church gets sucked into the same current and tends to lose the individual touch of the Master.

But at its best the church is always individual and personal. So in the sacraments that are the church's lifeblood. When the church baptizes, the individual is center stage. Even when many are baptized, each must be touched, immersed, given a name, and anointed. The same for confirmation, which manifests added concern for the individual now grown to maturity in faith. How intimate and personal the eucharist! The community is there, even crowds of people, but at the moment of climax, the personal Jesus is given to each and every individual to be taken and kept in heart and life. Reconciliation may begin and end in community but, however some may object, it must be completed in a private encounter between priest and penitent. Marriage is each loving individual giving the sacrament to the other alone. In orders, as in baptism, each of the ordinandi is called by name, is touched by bishop and priests, is anointed, and receives individually the eucharist that his new power of love has helped to consecrate. In sickness and in death again one's own forehead and hands are anointed and one's own body and heart receives the eucharistic Lord in hope and trust.

If we look to the best of Christians we find this same individual love. What saint is there who did not, like Jesus, leave the multitude to go off in search of the single lost one? Saints past and saints present. I think of Mother Teresa's response to those who criticize her concern for the individual while, because of structural injustice, millions are marginal, sick, and dying: "One at a time." And I think of Damien on Molokai. He was priest, doctor, carpenter, plumber, policeman, and teacher for the community of lepers; but always careful to keep what distance he could between himself and them. Then in some dream by day or night the revelation came to him. What his people wanted most from him was not all or any of the above, but simply that he would *touch* them, each of them. Not love at a distance for all, but close and intimate for each.

This kind of love is meant to endure into eternity. Other religions may speak of final absorption into the divine when the individual no longer is. Christ's religion teaches otherwise. This side of the grave God's individual love for me demands and fosters my growth as a person, primarily so that on the other side I might continue to grow as such. After death I shall, if God's love has its way, be even more me than I am now. God will be all in all, but his being in me and I in him will, amazingly, make both of us greater, to his joy and mine. How to understand this? Impossible, really, until one begins to understand something of this great personal love God is and has for each of us.

If the individual is so prized by God what then of community? Jesus prayed, "May they all be one, just as, Father, you are in me and I am in you" (Jn 17:21). The mystical body — all of us together — not the lone individual seems God's will for us. This is emphasized by the contemporary church. The in-word is *communio*. The preachment concerns bodies of people: the poor, the marginal, the oppressed, the blacks, hispanics, senior citizens, youth — all plural, collective, abstract words demanding *group* concern and action. Sin itself, rather than being individual, is collective, institutional: not *mea culpa* as once we declared in our common worship, but the sin and failure of church and world.

Community *is* our goal, but it is to be a community of individuals; the community fosters the growth and happiness of the individuals who compose it and who in turn promote and nourish the community. Individual and community are meant to grow together, but always the individual is central. Why, for instance, do I want to be part of my Dominican family? Originally it was that *I* might be helped thereby to draw closer to God. In the old parlance it was "to save my immortal soul," in this life and for the next. This has remained my deepest concern as far as I can judge. But I also want to save the other, to help him or her draw closer to God and the personal fulfillment to be found in God.

In both cases the individual is my concern — myself and the other. But the communal is also at work: the group's support, nourishment, teaching, tradition, and demands enable me to deepen my life in the Lord; my love and concern for individuals require that I make the same values and aids available to them. Love, always a communal affair, demands that I take lone, often lonely, isolated individuals and make love, and therefore community, a reality for them. My aim is the best for the individual and out of this springs the best of community. Should I, however, reverse priorities, then the community

becomes nonsense at best and monstrous at worst: individual
and community are both lost.

We must, like Christ and his true disciples through the
ages, be wary of words and concepts such as *group*, *world*,
nation, *social* justice, even *family* and *community*. They are to
be respected and fostered, but only as a means toward helping
create and re-create the individual. If regarded as such then
community becomes so beautiful that it may even appear to
be the end-all and be-all of everything. I would say that Jesus,
and St. Paul after him, had this in mind when they glorified
unity and the mystical body. The church, too, extols this ideal
when it accentuates community, though few, even within the
church, may realize it.

How is it, Lord, that you can and do love individual me?
How is it that, as Catherine of Siena put it, you're mad, drunk
with love for me? Catherine was puzzled by your love because
she felt unworthy. While I, too, often feel unclean, unworthy
of any love at all — especially yours — a greater problem is
that I can't grasp how out of all the billions of people who
are and have been you can single me out as though I were the
only one in your life, the alpha and omega of all your love,
and do the same with others, *all* others. St. Augustine said
that you love all as though one and one as though all. How
can this be? That's my problem.

It's a head problem: my little brain trying to understand the
mystery of your love which is the scarcely touchable mystery
of you yourself. But head often gets in the way of heart and
so it becomes a heart problem too: Though my heart believes
in your love for me, my belief is less than enthusiastic! I
wonder how many others who profess to be personally loved
and saved by you scarcely if at all truly believe it.

Part of my problem is that since human love is made in the
image of your divine love I tend to think of your love solely

in terms of mine: As I and the rest of humanity love, so do you. But, says the great philosopher Aristotle, speaking of the rarity of friendship, though I may have a broad, impersonal love for the many, I can love intensely only one or two. I imagine your personal love must likewise be limited.

Your love, however, is infinitely diverse from mine. Certainly in quantity: The magnitude of your love relative to mine is like my love at its best compared to that of an amoeba. But also it differs in quality, in *kind*. When I love I love from the outside in. I must first see the person, listen to her and listen to her listening to me. I must get within and behind her words and gestures, uncover her history, her hopes, dreams, joys, sorrows, and she must do the same with me. We must live, joy, suffer together. But all of this takes time, too much time to permit more than just one or possibly two or three to enter the fullness of my love. "Ah, love, let us be true to one another. . ." and let the rest find and live their own private loves.

But your love is from the inside out. You begin where other lovers hope at long last to arrive. You don't need time or space to get to know me or anyone else. You and your love are where I most am, and are there from the very beginning. Your love is the very heart of my own love and of all who love me; it is my very self in all my growth within and toward you. You and I are always and intimately alone.

I went to the beach at Santa Cruz the other day. The sun was full and warm and hundreds of people were basking in it, including myself. I felt its warmth along with the soft breeze that stirred now and again and cooled me off. I closed my eyes and felt as though the sun and breeze were for me alone, so lovingly was I touched by them. But when I opened my eyes I knew they were also for each bather on that beach as though he or she were exclusively there. It was the same when I dipped into the ocean. It was all mine and I alone was for it.

But how many others there felt the same! Then, in my mind, I placed the sun and the breeze and the ocean within me, and there I found you and your kind of love, my God! Loving me from within as though I were all in all, and loving all others in the same whole and happy way.

Isn't this the way of your saints? They practice your kind of loving, so they seem not to need time for love. Their love is immediate, intense, and unlimited, for like yours it begins from within. I think of St. John Vianney. Apparently penitents scarcely needed to speak their conscience since he seemed to know their sin and pain better than they themselves. I think of St. Thérèse of Lisieux, not just in her love for that unseen, unknown criminal, but in her passionate desire to love *all* and spend her heaven doing good on earth for each and every child of yours.

How I would like to love in this way! In the rare times that I do, my problem with your individual, personal love lessens or even vanishes altogether. More prayer, more sinking of my spirit into the Spirit of your love, and more grit effort at loving your kind of love might help here. And, above all, more patience in waiting for it to happen.

Christianity for me is also a matter of truth. "In the beginning was the Word" — the *Logos*, wisdom, truth in which all creation is grounded and out of which it originally arose. "I am the way, the *truth*, and the life," said Jesus, and declared that truth would set us free. I've thought so much about this through the years. I've had to. Truth is, after all, the watchword of the Order that has been my life for so long. But truth has also been a principal concern because I so often find the lie in my life. What a terrible thing to have to say, "I am a liar," especially when truth is one's public commitment. I keep trying to work against it; I keep trying to be true. One of the ways I've done this is through preaching, which, for me, is first a matter of facing — and facing up to — the truth myself and then inviting others to do the same. I may be a liar, but I know that I am, which is a piece of the truth, and maybe even the beginning of fullness of truth somewhere down the line.

How I wish I could become one with the meditation on truth that in one form or another I've several times preached to others of my Dominican family. . . .

The prime and essential concern of our Order from Dominic on has been the Word of God, the *Logos* that was in the beginning: in whom, through whom, with whom all things were made, all things stand and move, and all will be finalized. Thus our aim is truth — not this or that particular truth, but truth unlimited, wherever, however it may be found. Our emphasis has been upon religious truth, but only because truth itself demands such emphasis. But our ultimate orientation is toward all truth, the totality that is found in the Word of God.

Lest one think that having so broad a goal we have none at all, let me outline the particular attitudes and efforts that a dedication to truth might and should engender. First of all, it should engender openness of mind; and not *just* openness (which is often the slothful's excuse for believing absolutely nothing), but restlessness to know, with the confidence that if we seek we shall find. We may not be skeptics, agnostics, cynics; no intellectual despair is permitted us. And, since all truth is our province, we must move slowly. Hasty and thoughtless action cannot be ours, for we have to consider the whole, and that takes time. We must be patient in a restless world that has made change, not truth, its goal. This doesn't mean that we do not act, though failure to act is one of the hazards of our dedication, but it does mean that our action is to be thoughtful, considered, and true in itself, regardless of expediency or ultimate end or public image.

Does this make us conservatives and traditionalists? Yes, if there are past values which, according to the measure of truth, are worth preserving. Are we liberals? Yes, whenever truth demands change and transformation. Are we radicals? Could be, if once we've taken our measurements we find that according to truth we must tear down in order to raise up, destroy in order to build again. But always our orientation must be not to the new or the old, not to change or to the constant, neither to past values nor to present, but to truth.

Second, such dedication engenders a search that reaches far beyond the visible world. We have due reverence for intellect, but are not rationalists. We believe there is an order of truth beyond reason — contiguous to it, fundamentally in harmony with it, but above and beyond it. Within this order of "mystery" we must move, as well as within the visible and the rational.

Service to the truth demands our reverence for and involvement in the teaching church. In the interest of total truth, we can't run roughshod over considered declarations of pope and hierarchy. There may be confusion as to what is actually being taught by the church, and often there's call for legitimate doubt and denial. Certainly the considered thought of respected theologians also demands attention. But we cannot with impunity deny that some visible, audible remnant of Christ the teacher is left to us that alone can direct the human mind to reaches beyond itself. Here again we are forced to be patient and to move slowly — to give full consideration and weight to what ecclesiastical authority seriously proposes while at the same time recognizing that such proposals can only be the ground for our leap into what no eye has seen or ear heard or heart known or felt. The world of spirit is divine, but it is also satanic. Precisely because our sense of truth alerts us to this, we are to be cautious, for ourselves and others, as we venture into this other world; we are to look for directives where, it seems, Christ would have us look.

Third, it teaches us to have particular respect for language. Language is meant to be the expression of truth. And more

— language is vitally and organically bound up with truth, which doesn't exist, really, except in language. Words, simple words, make or break truth. Thus truth is largely a matter of hunting for the right word and, when it's found, truth stands revealed. We should care for right words. We should avoid at all costs the lie, which is language deliberately set at odds with truth, the broken promise, which is truth betrayed, and the cliche, which is language dead and truth buried. We should know and love language, particularly our own — know its history, its genesis, structure, and particular genius, and know its literature. We should take special care to speak and write as accurately as we can, and to appreciate the beauty of language used well. Being dedicated to *the* Word of God we should labor to use all words well.

Fourth, it requires us to *be* true. As there is to be no lie in our speech, there should be no lie in our person. We are to be true to what we are, *all* of what we are — as human beings and individuals, as lay, religious, or priest, as men or women. We ought to be wary of mentally dividing ourselves into parts or pieces: me as human being, me as individual, me as religious, me as male, etc. If we should deny or neglect or distort anything of what we are, we are no longer being true, and our growth, if growth there should be, will be monstrous. Our effort should be to accept, harmonize, vitalize everything that we are, so that no one, not even ourselves, might even think to divide us. No easy task, certainly, and one that is perhaps only rarely realized in a lifetime. But our vocation to truth demands that we begin, persevere, and progress in it now.

Finally, it brings us into others in a way that is intimate and as complete as the rest of our vocation will allow. First, it brings us into Christ, and Christ as he is in the deepest recesses of his being, for equally with love Christ is truth. In and through Christ, truth's eternal dimension has been revealed; in and through him, truth emerges as a person, as the Son of

God. To be in love with truth, then, deeply and genuinely in love with it, means to be in love with Christ in his deepest heart, even though He might not yet be known by any other name. So our brother, Meister Eckhart, didn't scruple to say: "Truth is something so noble that if God could turn aside from it, I could keep to the truth and let God go."

In kinship with the spirit of Eckhart, Mohandas Gandhi, the holy Hindu whose reverence for Jesus was profound, wrote: "I would say to those who say God is Love, God is Love. But deep down in me I used to say that though God may be Love, God is Truth above all. If it is possible for the human tongue to give the fullest description of God I have come to the conclusion that for myself, God is Truth. But two years ago I went a step further and said that Truth is God."

One of the most striking statements on the matter of devotion and faithfulness to the truth in its relevance to the Person of Christ was made by a woman of our time who was a Jewess, but a Christian in her deepest longing, though she refused, even to her death, to be baptized — Simone Weil. Speaking of her refusal to finally and fully embrace Christianity she wrote: "Yet I still half refused, not my love but my intelligence. For it seemed to me certain, and I still think so today, that one can never wrestle enough with God if one does so out of pure regard for the truth. Christ likes us to prefer truth to him because, before being Christ, he is truth. If one turns aside from him to go toward the truth, one will not go far before falling into his arms." Herein lies the beginning of a mystical encounter with truth, beyond reason, even beyond faith, in what St. Thomas would, I think, call the Spirit's "gift of wisdom."

Now that we have the revelation that truth is a person, every person becomes my truth. What is truth? You are my truth, and you, and you. We must try to know and understand everyone we meet, what they say or want to say, what they are, what they may become. We want to understand the universe.

Good. But let's remember that the highest truth, after God (but in God) is in the persons of those who people the universe.

We must, then, hesitate at times even to speak the truth for fear that it might harm someone who is our higher truth. We must never dissociate truth from charity, for *the* truth is the great God of Love. Truth itself does sometimes require that we keep it silent. We must also tolerate and respect the opinions of others. They may not have the truth as we see it, may not have the truth as it is; but as long as they are honestly searching, they are to have our respect and courtesy. We can and should argue, state our position honestly and vigorously as need requires; but humbly, too — we are often wrong when we most think we're right — and with deepest reverence for the person of the one with whom we are arguing. He or she may be the most important truth in any argument.

"The mystical dimension of truth. . ." There's so much talk today of mysticism. This is good, because there had been blessed little talk of it in the church in recent times. Protestants, except for some notable exceptions, had long since abandoned it and Catholics for the most part knew very little about it. It seems that only with the propagation of oriental modes of religious awareness and discipline was the Catholic church shamed into reaching back into her past and offering laity, as well as clergy and religious, her own rich tradition of mystical prayer. That tradition is rooted in Christ himself, his life and his teaching, and has been lived and developed in a variety of ways by holy men and women through the centuries. What follows may be a fair summary of the bare bones of the church's tradition seen in the context of mysticism in general and as it relates to the mysticism of some oriental religions.

First, mysticism as it appears in venerated mystics of both east and west involves an intense awareness of "divinity," "the

other side," the "numinous" or "transcendent." The mystic
sees the numinous first and always, and sees all other things
in and through it, while others see things first, and only now
and again penetrate to the divine, and they see the divine in
the light and after the fashion of visible things. The same
holds true on the level of action. The mystic is aware of God
acting in the world while he or she helps to fulfill or frustrate
the divine action. Others see themselves as acting — see the
world or some part of it as dependent upon them — and now
and again they may pray to God for help. In the one case God
is the doer with our help; in the other we are the doers with
or without God. This fundamental passivity of the mystic,
however, often yields an energy and an action that is swift,
penetrating, fruitful, and lasting.

A second characteristic of mysticism is consequent upon
the first: the primacy of spirit over matter, the indisputable
supremacy of the invisible underlying oneness and constancy
over all too visible change and diversity. In the east the latter is
maya (illusion) and the deep invisible self *is* the *atman* (God
within). In Christian mysticism, while matter may amount to
considerably more and self considerably less than in the east,
still the spirit or soul, the interior castle, the kingdom within
is prized, and all else is profitable only in terms of it. So the
mystic sees where others do not and cares for what others
tend to ignore, and is much more aware of eternity than of
time, of the hidden, giant *now* that survives the ticking of the
clock.

A third characteristic of mysticism is asceticism or yoga.
Discipline is necessary for the attainment of anything worthwhile and is certainly evidenced in the serious pursuit of any
of the arts or sciences. Blood, sweat and tears, as well as joy
and laughter, are products of every venture into the unknown;
if we would have one great thing, often we have to surrender many lesser goods. So it is with the *scientia sanctorum*.
Those who set out to achieve it must train — "mortify" — the

totality of their person as rigorously as athletes must train their mind and body or scientists and artists their vision and imagination. They must themselves surrender many things (active purgation) and suffer themselves to be deprived of still more (passive purgation). Many of us subject ourselves or are subjected to some of the discipline. Mystics, as the great artists, scholars, and athletes, go the whole way. Their discipline is total and unrelenting that their vision and love might be full.

These are general characteristics of mysticism. Accordingly, they are found in Christian mysticism, but modified according to Christian belief and as part of a more complex whole. First, Christian mysticism is centered upon Jesus Christ, who is both God and a man, one Person who is both human and divine. Thus, as always with the mystics, the divine is central, but the human, and through the human the whole of the visible world, is of "dear worth," both as goal and means: They become "the way" into the divine and the object or goal of a divinely transformed love. For those whose mysticism is rooted in Jesus Christ the world can never be *maya* nor can it be simply a means to an end. And so, although the Christian mystic may leave the world for a time, may even "despise" it, in order to draw closer to God in purity and freedom, he or she must always, in act or in affection, return to the world, love it, work in and for it, and offer it anew to the Father.

Secondly, asceticism for the Christian mystic must be tempered in the light of the centrality of Jesus Christ. This follows from the above: Since the body of the world is *real* and is a goal of love as well as a means toward love, it must not be maltreated or suppressed, but rather reverenced and perfected. It also follows from two of the three great mysteries of Christianity, the Incarnation and Resurrection. By the former, God reaches down to us, dwells among us, is near at hand, is incarnated in the visible world around us, in our very flesh. Thus the effort to find and hold him is lessened, since he has already found us. By the Resurrection, even the fallen

elements of the world demand our respect and care, are not to
be cast off but raised with the risen Christ. Even sin is not to
be rejected out of hand, but transformed: "Though your sins
are like scarlet, they shall be white as snow" (Is 1:18). Thus
in Christian mysticism the positive aspects of asceticism are
stressed: It becomes the effort and consequent pain required
in transforming and elevating a fallen self and world — a
creative labor of love.

The third great mystery of Christianity, the Trinity, is responsible for two other special characteristics of Christian
mysticism. Because God is one, the Christian mystic shares
with mystics of the east a profound sense of the oneness and
constancy of a universe reflective of this one God. But because *within* the one God there is an ineffable diversity of
persons — a diversity, indeed, that is infinite as everything
in God is infinite — the Christian mystic parts company with
her eastern counterpart. God is one, but also plural; and so
the world, reflective of him, is both one and many, constant
and deeply at rest, but also changing and demanding change,
forever restless and becoming new. The Christian mystic sees
and loves this fullness and revels in the paradox and mystery
of it all: "Glory be to God for dappled things . . ." the many,
diverse things "He fathers forth whose beauty is past change."
The eastern mystic, on the other hand, can only lament diversity and long for the spiritual and psychological state in which
all diversity vanishes and absolute oneness alone remains.

This infinite diversity within and outside God is also responsible for the Christian mystic's emphasis upon love. Love
becomes possible only where there is diversity: It takes at
least two to make love, and many to make even greater love!
Christian mysticism is communal — familial, social, politi-
cal — not just in its beginnings but in term and ideal; and
the oneness it aims at is not the solitary absolute unity that
is the goal of eastern mysticism but union and harmony in
love. Love is certainly part of the vocabulary and life of the

eastern mystic, but it's something along the way. For him the great virtue is knowledge or wisdom, the *gnosis*; and above all he is the *guru* or teacher. The Christian mystic also values and manifests wisdom and often becomes the teacher *par excellence*, but her greatest virtue is *caritas* and her wisdom — the greatest gift of the Spirit — is such because it is a *loving* knowledge or vision. She is above all a lover and remains such unto eternity where she revels as a full and fully developed person distinct from God and others but intimately united to them in a bond of understanding, peace, and joy. But we must stress that it's not a superficial, merely social kind of love that characterizes the Christian mystic, but a love that wells up *de profundis* — out of the depths of the solitude of the one God. Aloneness and love are not opposites. Rather one is the indispensable condition of the realness and depth of the other.

I don't want to suggest by this contrast between eastern and western (Christian) mysticism that individual mystics of either tradition don't share in the special characteristics of the other. There has been mutual influence throughout a long history, and as there have been eastern mystics with Christian bent so there have been Christian mystics who manifest eastern tendencies. But Christianity, at least in its Catholic expression, with its strong traditional accent upon doctrine and dogma, has educated and disciplined its mystics to live, pray, and serve according to its specific teaching. As instanced by such diverse lovers of the Lord as Hildegaard of Bingen, Thomas Aquinas, Meister Eckhart, Catherine of Siena, Teresa of Avila, John of the Cross, Ignatius Loyola, Bartolomeo de las Casas, Thérèse of Lisieux, Maximilian Kolbe, and Dorothy Day, that teaching has been of salutary service to them and, through their vitalization and expansion of it, has benefitted the rest of the world as well.

FIVE

The Spirit
and the Woman

As any work of any maker, all creation is a reflection of its maker God who, in the Christian perspective, is one in nature and multiple in person. Thus the infinite multiplicity of things, species, forces, individuals in the world, and yet the tantalizing unity that demands that we name this world of ours a *universe*: all things converging into one. Thus also our appreciation of and care for different individual persons while also valuing and promoting the family, community, state, nation, with our longing for one world, a league or union of nations, a family of the families of humankind.

But creation reflects the triune God in a more specific way, that is, specific to each person of the Trinity. Because of their absolute oneness, all creation is the product of the whole Trinity, each divine person lovingly, generously involved in the work of the other; yet each has a specific nuance, some particular contribution to the overall work. The fact, for instance, that things are, exist — that's the Father who with the others, though more deeply than they, brings things out of nothing and holds them in being. His particular work is existential. The fact that things are ontologically true, that they cry out to be known — that's the Son, the Word according to whom all things are formed and fashioned and revealed. His work is intellective. The fact that things move, stir, desire and are desired — that's the Spirit whose special work is love. The Holy Spirit is the loving heart of Father and Son, as of all the life and love of the universe.

All movement, all life is from the Spirit. The very word — *spiritus* in Latin, *pneuma* in Greek, *ruach* in Hebrew — means breath, and breath is the sign of life. If we want to know if someone is alive we ask, "Is he breathing?" We speak of a spirited horse or of someone who has "plenty of spirit" and in each case we have vitality, life in mind. The scriptures testify to the Spirit's life-giving action. At the genesis of all, as the Father calls things into being in and according to his Word ("And God *said* . . .") so it is the Spirit, the Breath of God, *ruach Elohim*, hovering, moving, brooding over the chaotic waters, who stirs and warms them into life as a brooding hen her chicks. When God formed Adam he "breathed into his nostrils the breath of life, and so Adam became a living being." When Christ, the new Adam, was formed he was "conceived," given life by the Spirit, hovering over Mary as at the beginning of the first creation. Then in the third creation, that of the church, it is the Spirit again, as flashing flames and a mighty wind, the breath of nature as well as of God, who stirs the disciples into new life. And throughout those first years of the church the Spirit's life and love continue to provoke the prodigious *vitality* of the church.

The Holy Spirit's also called the "spirit of truth." Christ, the Son, is Truth, but, according to Christ himself, something more than just truth is needed. At his final banquet of love he tells his disciples that he must go away so that the Paraclete, "the Spirit of Truth," might come and guide them to all truth. Christ "out there," as objective, historical truth is not enough — that knowledge has to be animated, made living within us. It is the Spirit within who does this, who "keeps our metaphysics warm," who gives life and urgency to truth, keeps it full and real, one with our life and all life: truth in total context!

It's not too difficult, then, dear Spirit, to recognize you as the dynamic center of all movement, life, love of the universe. Your poet, Dante, at the conclusion of his great poem sings of "the Love that moves the sun and other stars." And so I look up into the stars and as they're born, burst, speed through an infinity of space I find you. I look to the ebb and flow of ocean, rivers, lakes and I find you. And if I could see deep into the atom I'd find you there too, whirling its particles through inner space as the stars through outer.

It's you who gives *me* life, love, and movement. When, early in our morning I lie dormant, no life in me, reluctant to leave womb or bed, you prod me with: "Time to get up and get going." At the noon of life, when the noonday devil would divert me into *his* way, you urge me to keep on course. At twilight, when I'm tired of it all and want to have done, you tell me of the miles to go before I sleep. And at nightfall, when sleep at last is forced upon me, you'll be most there (I hope!) to move me across the threshold into new life and love.

Your special job is also to unite since it's through movement, particularly that of love, that things lying apart draw together. Thus you're the link between Father and Son, the one who eternally draws and binds them together. You're deeply present in the church, especially in times of crisis, often making the crisis, shaking things up, unbinding what has become rigid and lifeless, scattering, but only to draw together again into a more vital, loving union. Church councils, so disturbing at times, and ecumenism, often shattering our set thoughts and ways, are from and of you. You break up the old but only that a new union be formed reflective of your own triune life.

I don't mean to imply that you're behind all revolutions and any kind of movement and action. There's movement that's superficial, action off the top of one's head, and revolutions that are angry, violent, and destructive. What do you, the depth of God, the dove of peace, the gentle mother of

creation have to do with any of this? To the extent that action is thoughtless (lacking in the Word) and revolution, even
when just, is more angry than loving, destructive rather than
creative, you are absent, and filling the void is that other spirit
who comes from below. Your kind of action is rooted in prayer
and deep pondering on your revelation. Before ever he began
his revolution, before, perhaps, he even knew of it, Jesus was
led by *you* into the desert to fast and pray and face himself
and what was to come; in short to surrender himself completely to the Father. It is you, then, who continually lead us
into the desert, there to watch and pray with Jesus, that we
might enter into *his* action and so help bring *both* justice and
peace to our world.

Had we the eyes for it we'd see the light of the Spirit
reflected in the dynamic of every particle of creation from
megastar to microphoton, from the imperceptible glacial
movement of mountains to the much less perceptible light-
ning movement of mind and heart, from the breakup of the
old to the birth of the new, from visible active ministry before
the world to hidden, quiet prayer in desert or cloister.

But there's still another presence of the Spirit that we miss,
much more personal and intimate than any of the others —
that embodied in the woman called Mary. With the Spirit, the
Spirit through her, she mothers the church, the new creation,
as the Spirit mothered the old creation and ancient Israel. "The
Holy Spirit will come upon you, and the power of the Most
High will cover you with its shadow. And so the child will
be holy and will be called Son of God" (Lk 1:35).

When I think of God's love I think of it in terms of a
mother's love — the most clinging, constant, tenacious, crazy
love I or anyone else knows. It's a love that's there before

you're born, even conceived; it's there, protecting, nourishing you in every waking and sleeping moment of your infancy and young childhood; it abides and even deepens as you move into adolescence; and, wonder of wonders, it persists as you marry, grow old, sin, fail, are in disgrace. All others might abandon you, and rightly so, but it's a rare mother who will ever abandon her child, however young, however old, however evil.

When I think of a mother's love I think of my own mother, of course, and of Mary, Jesus' mother and mine, but also I think of Maureen. Once she came to visit me with the child I had baptized. As the child crawled about, Maureen and I talked of different things. Then she paused, looked down at her baby, and apropos of nothing said: "Why is it that I love him so?" And her eyes were filled with love! I had a sudden inspiration and said: "Why don't we talk about it? Why do you think you love him?" For the next hour we talked about it. Here's the gist of what she said as I jotted it down after she had left:

> I love him because he's so much a part of me. For a while he *was* me, so that I could scarcely distinguish my body from his. And whatever I do for him it's like doing it for myself, and whatever I do for myself is for him. How totally one we are!
>
> Yet I love him because he's so different from me. So much of me and John within him, and yet he's full of surprises! More than once John and I have said to each other: "Where in the world did he get that from: that pouting lip, that extraordinary smile? And those fits of temper? Must be from your side of the family!" And yet we both know it's from neither side. Little Johnny is his own man, and there's little we can, or want, to do about it.
>
> I love him because he's the fruit, the expression of the love between John and me. It's so difficult at times for us to express that love. Really, there's more frustration here than anything. Such clumsiness in trying to say

"I love you," and even more in trying to show it. But when Johnny's in bed with us, lying between us, then neither of us has to say or do anything. It's a perfect trinity, and we need no further proof of our love.

And I love him, I guess, because he's so helpless. He depends on me for everything — for food, shelter, clothing, love, affection. If for the briefest time I should forget to tend him or have him tended to he might slip away from life itself or be severely wounded. Oh, Father, I've changed his diapers so many times, and each time I've done so my love for him has deepened!

After Maureen left I thought long and hard about what she had said, and, as you know, Lord, I thought of it in terms of your love for me. Why do *you* love *me* so? I suppose it's because I'm so much a part of you: breath of your breath, life of your life, begotten in your image and likeness. What you do for yourself you do for me, and in loving me you're loving yourself. Yet I'm so different from you, full of surprises, and often not very pleasant ones. Yet you love me even more for being my own man; as though this is why you made me: to be one with you and yet infinitely different.

You love me because I'm the visible expression of the love within yourself — Father, Son, and Holy Spirit — as though looking upon me in the folly of love you say to each other: "See the fruit of our love. Isn't our love wonderful!" And yes, you love me because I'm so helpless. Remove but for an instant your loving hand from mine and I slip not just from life but from existence itself. And how many diapers of mine have you changed through the years! All my sin and failure, all the waste of my life. Yet, you love me all the more, if not because of it then certainly in spite of it.

Lord, I'm not aware of any of this great love of yours for me, any more than little Johnny crawling about my room was aware of his mother's love for him. But that doesn't cancel out the love; it simply invites me to look more carefully, more deeply for the great mother's love you have for me and for all of us.

Has Mary been lost to our contemporary world? Hardly, when tens of millions annually visit her many shrines throughout the world and many millions more pray with and to her within confines of home, parish, diocese. But she's also present among us in less obvious ways and, surprisingly perhaps, in ways close to the heart of contemporary society.

We think of the presence or absence of Mary, as of Jesus, in terms of visibility or of imaginable or intelligible content. Thus if there's a dearth of "thinking" about Mary or of images of her, we would say that she is absent in our time; on the contrary we would say she was present in former times, especially in the medieval and early renaissance worlds, when she was quite visible in the content of theology, art, architecture, poetry, music.

But there's another kind of presence: invisible, unconscious, the presence of form rather than content, the kind of presence we're asked to look for, say, in nonrepresentational art or in music, or in poetry where the music or rhythm precedes idea and image and helps create them. This is a presence of thrust, of dynamic, of spirit . . . like that of the Spirit of God hovering over the yet unformed waters of chaos and warming them toward visibility and life.

Perhaps Mary is present here and there in our time in this last manner. If we would find her and her possible influence upon contemporary culture we should look in this direction as well as in that of visible content. In fact, this is the direction in which we should seek to define culture itself. Culture is not a matter of any one specific content or subject or activity nor of all taken enmasse. Rather, it's the inherited dynamism or spirit or form that produces each of them in all their various nuances, though it itself is affected and reshaped by them. The same is true with regard to God and Jesus: it's not so much the content of our thought about them, not the images we have of them, that's telling, but what underlies these, beyond thought and image, inspiring and shaping the content of our belief.

I think of Mary in a similar way. In the earliest church there was not, perhaps, much content or visibility of Mary, at least when compared to Jesus and his male disciples, to Paul and his entourage. But, to borrow an image from one of her later lovers, it seems she was there from beginning to end as "atmosphere," as "world-mothering air," as form or spirit shaping the emerging thought and action of the church. Certainly it was in her modest context, her "atmosphere," that Christ was preserved from mere myth and acknowledged as substantially and earthily human (so Paul's almost casual aside: "born of a woman"). By the late Middle Ages and early Renaissance that spirit had blossomed into a fullness of content. Then that content began to harden till in some instances and locales it quenched the moving spirit and became *identified* with Mary. And could it be that Vatican II tried to recover her spirit, her "form"? If so, we must not mistake what it had to say about Mary for the fullness of Mary but, with its beginnings, refocus on the thrust of Mary in our time and beyond.

Speaking of Mary's presence in this way suggests another presence, that of the Holy Spirit. St. Maximilian Kolbe spoke boldly of Mary as the "quasi-incarnation" of the Holy Spirit, emphasizing the latter part of this hyphenation. Since then less venturesome theologians have accentuated the *quasi*. In any case few Catholic theologians will deny Mary's special and intimate relationship with the Spirit. They go hand in loving hand, indissolubly wedded. Not only because they were cooperatively together at the conception of Christ and later at the birth of the church, but because they have a kind of natural affinity. Both are hidden, in the background as it were, but dynamically so, strikingly re-emerging at critical moments in Jesus's adult years — as when the Spirit leads Jesus into the desert to prepare him for his ministry, and when Mary, waiting for Jesus "apart from the crowd," inspires in him the revolutionary declaration as to his true and lasting kindred (Mk 3:31–35). I think of other characteristics shared by the Spirit and Mary, and discoverable in certain movements or thrusts of our time.

There's the interiorization of religion. Certainly the subjective aspect of belief and morality is emphasized today. Even those who rightly uphold the objectivity of belief and morals are concerned more than ever with liberty of conscience, personal and cultural limitations of understanding, the virtue of prudence and its largely intuitive functioning, the uniqueness of a given "situation," and the restoration in one form or another of casuistry (the individual case). But interiorization, subjectivity, and intuition are of the unpredictable Spirit who blows where he wills and of the traditionally feminine rather than of the predictable and predicting rational and the traditionally masculine. Purged of all excess and distortion they are, in other words, of the Holy Spirit and Mary.

There's the resurgence of contemplative prayer. In the last twenty to thirty years there has been in the western world a mounting interest in and practice of meditative prayer, sparked by eastern imports such as TM, Zen, Yoga, and now developed along lines of traditional Christian contemplation. This prayer is seen to be not just for the select few, mainly among nuns and monks, but for everyone in whatever walk of life. This is another aspect of interiorization and the letting go of content in favor of a poised and expectant darkness. It is looking not to what is outside (image, word, symbol, creed) but to what is within, to the private, personal "revelation," to what God is "saying" to *me* here and now — like a pregnant woman turned inward, quietly aware of the mystery growing within her. Here again is the Holy Spirit praying within us when, as St. Paul tells us (Rom 8:26–27), we don't know what to pray for (that is, when all content is surrendered) and here is Mary, the silent, pondering, surrendering contemplative par excellence. Unseen, unfelt, they are at the heart of so many today who are trying to pray such a prayer, and so many others feeling the need of it — if only to avoid being torn apart and scattered by the noise and confusion of a world off-center.

Another mark, and need, of our world today is ecumenism, conceived now as the unification not just of the various Christian churches but of all the world religions. Again we may see here the stirring of the Spirit who is the bond of love, the *vinculum caritatis*, uniting Father and Son, the creative presence hovering over the deep, bringing, at the Father's *Word*, order out of chaos, the one forming and securing the one church in the beginning. And as Mary, with and in the Spirit, conceived and brought to birth the one undivided Christ, so her labor today joins the Spirit with regard to the church. I know many Catholic theologians today would have us downplay Mary so as not to offend their Protestant brothers and sisters and thereby impede ecumenism. I should think it would be just the opposite, providing the depth of Mary is presented, which is her spirit, her form more than her traditional content; though the latter, in the *purity* of church teaching and practice, is of marked importance too, for itself and for what it reveals of her spirit and the new directions that spirit may take, for all the churches, in the future.

There's today's concern for social justice. Whereas in former times we would speak of charity and the works of charity, now the cry is for justice and the doing of justice: We do for the poor not so much out of our love and their need as out of our sense of justice and their rights. Again, in the past justice has been in the main the province of the male, the one actively engaged in the world, in politics, business, civil defense, etc. But women are more and more coming to the fore in it, seeking justice for themselves and for the marginal and oppressed in general.

Here's a fresh dynamic of Mary, the seed of which, however, was there from the beginning. Those writing of Mary today, particularly women, view her in the context of the women of justice in the ancient Hebrew world — Esther, Deborah, Judith —and see a whole theology of social justice in Mary's *Magnificat*. If the movement toward social justice is of the Holy Spirit, who as creative love seeks balance, harmony, substantial peace, and concord then, yes, we can find, if we look, the Spirit's consort at work with the Spirit toward the same goal. Mary, while drawing us within in contemplative stillness, also directs us outward to the Christ who lived and lives in our objective, tangible world and identified himself with the quite visible poor and needy. She points to *this* Christ dwelling outside us as well as within; so too does the Holy Spirit who, as the gospel tells us, is there to remind us continually of all Christ has visibly done and audibly spoken. Perhaps part of the new "content" of Mary today is this visibility of the woman in works of justice and peace, not as having lost the interiorization, the contemplative spirit, the gentle, mothering love of her past, but as gaining something in addition: the hidden life come forth openly to help heal the world while paradoxically still remaining hidden. Mary remains what she was in the past and *therefore* under the press of current need becomes someone new for the present.

When considering Mary in her relationship to women, past and present, we must be careful. Christ is male; his maleness is part of his history, and history is important in Christianity. But his maleness is meant mainly as a means of access to his humanity and person which are neither male nor female. Christ is equally for both men and women, though, of course, in different ways according to different psychologies and cultures.

However, the historical fact of Christ's maleness has often dominated our thinking about him, with regretful results, as when, in spite of social changes it is used to justify an ongoing exclusively male ecclesiastical leadership. Similarly with Mary: Her femininity is a providential part of her history, but she is of greater moment as a human being and person. Accordingly she is for the man as well as the woman; she serves both equally and both are to learn from her, though, again, in different ways.

Yet her femininity has had its influence, for good and bad. For bad, it has tended to limit our ideal of the Christian woman to what it was in Mary's own day and to which, accordingly, she herself was in good measure bound. For good, it has softened our conception of God and so made our approach to him easier, more inviting, loving rather than fearful. In and through the gospels, through the art, poetry, and drama of the ages, seeing God in the arms and in the care and "power" of this then insignificant Jewish woman, quiet, gentle, lowly, we find some of that same womanhood rubbing off, as it were, on Father God. A fair part of the accessibility of Jesus himself, his merciful compassion, is the fact that he has Mary as his flesh-and-blood mother. Without her, would we be altogether convinced of the mercy of God and the understanding compassion of Jesus? Here is one way in which the "content" or dogma of Mary has affected us in the past, with its mark still upon us, thankfully. In the present thrust of woman toward justice, with Mary behind (and before) her, it would be tragic if this content were surrendered in favor of one that is hard, merely active, superficially and imitatively masculine. Eventually God himself might regress into the terror and cruelty of past and present dark religions.

Mary can be looked upon in two ways. Undeniably she is a historical person, flesh and blood, the daughter of parents tradition names Anna and Joachim, the physical, natural mother of Jesus. Here she is all and only human. But she must also be seen as symbol, the special kind of symbol that makes present in very reality what it symbolizes. As the eucharist does not simply remind us of Christ but makes him really present upon our altars, so Mary doesn't simply recall the Holy Spirit to our minds and point us in the Spirit's direction; she makes the Spirit really present among and within us. Seeing her we see the Spirit, as seeing the eucharist we see Christ himself. This is a good and legitimate reason for addressing the Spirit as feminine — not as a sop for the marginal woman but simply because just as there are reasons for addressing God as Father or Son there is this equally cogent reason for addressing God as Mother. As in time, in the mystery of the Incarnation there is eternal Father, mother Mary, and Son Jesus, so in eternity there is Father and Son with mothering Spirit as their bond of love.

Let me, Mary, become young and foolish again, just for a nostalgic moment. Remember when years ago I prayed before your statue in the novitiate grove and made my vows to you even before I made them publicly in chapel? You were my lady, and I your knight about to enter upon years of adventure to prove my love for you. I remember the sunlight slanting through the redwoods, the light playing upon you, with you. I recall, too, the mosquitoes trying to distract me from you, but to no avail. They served only to deepen my prayer, make it real as well as romantic, prayer not outside the harsh world but crying within it to you and the great Spirit of the world within, around, and beyond both of us.

You were my love then, Mary. I'm old now, and tired. But you're still my love, my life. You're not as alone in my thought as you were in my young years. You're rather there, like God, with everyone, everything else — the deep waters, the wellspring that underlies all, feeds and nourishes all. I don't *think* of you as much anymore, but I'm *aware* of you always. Like my very life you're alive within me whether I'm awake or asleep, whether I pray or sin; even when I doubt or deny you, God, everything, you're there, loving me and loved by me. You're my lady still, and I your wandering knight.

Then, Mary, there was that other vision of you. It was at beautiful Carmel during retreat with my students. That first morning I rose early to get my own prayers in before helping the retreatants with theirs. It was a warm morning with just enough light to see my way by as I walked the crescent of the beach to the heaped-up rocks at its end. I climbed out onto the rocks and sat there and prayed, or rather listened to the prayer of sky and ocean, gull and heron. Then I looked down into the pool of crystal water beside me, onto the stones and shells that sparkled beneath. I selected several of the more precious ones, held them in my hands, meditated and prayed over them, then put them in my pocket.

The rest of the day was filled with conferences, counseling, confessions, a "trust walk," liturgy, and all the other necessary things. I had forgotten all about the stones and shells, till bedtime. When I emptied my pockets I looked on them like strangers until I remembered our morning meeting. They were so different now. All the sparkle was gone from them. They were dull and commonplace. They were simply crusty stones and brittle shells. I knew what I had to do.

Next morning I rose early again and returned to my rock and crystal pool. I placed my treasures back in the pool, and lo and behold, they were alive again, they shimmered and sparkled, almost danced and sang in those clean, clear waters. It was then that I "saw" you. You were those waters, and

God was the stones and shells, and I realized what was meant when you said "My soul magnifies the Lord." You make God shine. I can't see you, don't even know you're there, you're so clean, clear, and quiet. But what I see of God, his sparkle and grace, is because I see him in and through you. Yes, you magnify the Lord, you actually add to him, make him pleasing, gentle, loving, beautiful in my sight. You add to him because you are part of him, the part that first touches me and brings me into his depth. You gave humanity to God, *your* humanity, the bright and glorious, singing and dancing, shining and sparkling flesh and blood of your Jesus. You are unseen, unnoticed, but in and through your transparent cleanness I have God, I love and worship him. My thanks to you, and him, for this.

SIX

Eucharist: Word and Words

From Christianity's earliest beginnings until now the center of its worship has been the eucharist. We might think back upon its distant foreshadowing in the gifts of Abel, the sacrifice of Abraham, the bread and wine offered by Melchisedek, and the paschal lamb. Several times through word and action Jesus seems to have promised the gift: At the beginning of his public life at Cana he changed water to wine — later he would change wine into his blood; he multiplied a few loaves and fishes to feed thousands — the time would come when he would feed the whole world with himself; he preached with point and poignancy on the bread of life — explicitly identifying himself with it.

But it was on the very eve of his passion — we might rather say the very beginning of it — that he gave us the gift, the better, I suppose, to impress upon us its magnitude. The last *act* of his life — for from then on it was all and only passion — was to give us himself in intimate and lasting communion. The Holy Spirit saw to it that the deed would be not only practiced and preached in the early church but duly recorded for all time. The three synoptic gospels and St. Paul narrate the Last Supper with explicit mention of the consecrating words of Jesus. The gospel of John, though without the eucharistic formula at the Last Supper, had already dwelt at length on Jesus as the bread of life and the need to eat his flesh and drink his blood. But also, at the supper itself, John shows Jesus revealing the internal meaning of the eucharist. The other evangelists and Paul declare the external, visible sacrament of the eucharist, John presents and probes its inward grace: "I am the vine, you are the branches. . . . As the Father has loved me, I also have loved you. Abide in my love. . . . This is my commandment, that you love one another as I have loved you. . . . Greater love than this no one has, than to lay down one's life for one's friends. . . . I pray that all may be one, even as you, Father, are in me and I in you, that they also may be one in us. . . . "

The church could not forget so clear, so emphatic, so loving a message. The eucharist has indeed been central, especially in the life of the Catholic church, not just as yearly, monthly, or weekly celebration, but daily. If you think of the church around the world, the celebration is even hourly: "From the farthest east to the farthest west my name is great among the nations, and everywhere incense and a pure gift are offered to my name" (Mal 1:11). Whatever the occasion — coronation of kings and queens, celebrations of victory, laments over defeats, graduations, marriages, ordinations, baptisms, births and deaths, in palaces, in prison camps, in cathedrals, in private homes, in public, in secret — the eucharist is celebrated and is climactic. Great buildings have been erected to house it, great art to embelish it, great poetry and music to probe and surround it. People have lived for it — have even lived in perpetual adoration before it — and people have died for it. Through the ages it has undergone changes, with different locales and cultures celebrating it in a variety of rites, but always the essentials of that first eucharist are there: the word of God in scripture and sermon; the offering of self and all to the Father; the transforming words of Jesus; communion with one another in and through the sacred bread and wine; and, in and through it all, thanksgiving.

What is it that makes the eucharist so great? Let's try for the beginnings of an answer.

First, the eucharist is Christ himself: "This is my body . . . my blood." It is Christ even more perfectly than when he walked our earth two thousand years ago. Then he was limited to a given place — Palestine, and at any given moment to only one of its villages or cities — and was bound by the calendar of his day. But in and through the eucharist he is wherever and whenever the eucharist is celebrated. Granted Jesus, like the God he is, is present everywhere and in all time independently of the eucharist. But as Dante begins his last and greatest poem: "He is in one place more and another less." There are intensifications of God's presence, and in the eucharist that presence is most intimate and intense.

Even more than this, the eucharist is Christ in his deepest act of love. Jesus said — and at the first eucharist — that we can have no greater love than to lay down our lives for our friends. Here, in the eucharist, Jesus does just this: "This is my body *which will be given up* for you. This is the cup of my blood *which will be shed* for you." So the Mass is Calvary itself — not a sacrifice distinct from Jesus' one and only sacrifice, but the way given us to sweep us up into that sacrifice of love, to make us mindful of it and grateful for it, to incorporate us into it with all our own crucifixions. It's like a window through which we can look back in time to those very moments when Christ cried, and still cries: "Father, forgive them, for they know not what they do." Christ's passion was temporal since his humanity bound him by space and time. But because even as a human being he is also God, his passion is eternal, transcending time and able to be present in every time. In and through the eucharist such presence is effected.

Still more, the eucharist is our way of becoming one with Christ in his great act of love. St. Augustine speaks of how when we eat ordinary bread it is changed into us — becomes our flesh, blood, bone. But when we eat *this* bread we are turned into it. We *become* the body of Christ. Augustine declares that when the minister says to a communicant, "Body of Christ," the phrase signifies that the *communicant* is that body, the very Body, I would add, hanging upon the cross for love of humankind. I may be a poor lover through most of my days, tepid, even cold and hard. But in the moments of eucharist, if I truly want to love, then I am a great lover, for now it is no longer I who lives and loves but Christ within me.

More even than this, the eucharist is our way of becoming one with one another in Christ's act of love. To paraphrase the early fathers: As from many grapes comes a single cup of wine and from many grains a single loaf of bread, so in the eucharist the scattered children of christendom are brought together into a single people. One of my great joys as a priest has been to celebrate Mass in a large inner-city church. There at communion time I would give the body of Christ to young and old, black, yellow, brown, white, people obviously well-off, others obviously poor, some apparently well-educated, others not, some Republicans, others Democrats, still others some party unto themselves or of no party at all. . . Yet all receive the same body of Christ and before him all are equal and equally loved.

Here, in the presence of the eucharist (whatever past and now forbidden discriminatory practice may have been) we are one, whatever we may be outside of it. Within the eucharist and the preaching that is an essential part of it division must not be provoked, as St. Paul had warned the Corinthians centuries ago. The eucharist and its preaching must be honest, timely, true to the new as well as the old; it must speak of justice as well as love to each of us in present circumstance. Yet it must not be divisive, for the simple reason that it is the last common ground where we can at least begin to think the thoughts and do the deeds that will make us one — or nearly so — outside the eucharist as well as within.

Out of all this and more that the eucharist is, many pick and choose. For some the eucharist is communion and community, table fellowship with one another in the Lord. For others it is a remembrance of Jesus, his life, death, and resurrection. Others believe it's Jesus himself, body, soul, and divinity. For others it's the unbloody sacrifice of Calvary. Fine. The eucharist is so big that we have to specialize when we think of it or we'll fail to think of it at all. As with stark divinity, we conceptualize it in different ways at different times, and different people in different cultures and religions variously conceive of it. But now and again we ought to at least allow for fullness, let our particular ideas go and leave ourselves open for *all* that God and his sacrament are. Otherwise we'll end up not with the eucharist but with some narrow superstition of our own making.

But is the eucharist really all that the scriptures imply and a long tradition has declared? I see, feel none of the greatness attributed to it. In fact the opposite is the case. It's so small, so fragile, and so brief a moment. What looks to be a bit of bread, a few drops of wine, some modest words and gestures, is declared to match the whole universe and God himself in magnitude. How can we believe this? When it's celebrated by ministers and congregations who are careless to the point of sacrilege, and when, as often happens, I take the eucharist out of its context of altar and church and bring it to homes unprepared for it and, apparently, unwilling to prepare for it, with chattering and television blasting away, I feel it may well be I, not the "irreverent" people, who am deceived.

But isn't this true of Christianity in general, and indeed of the whole of life? The most important things are those that are hidden away and unnoticed. I don't see the very air I breathe, seldom feel, hear, smell it, yet shut it off from me and it's not long before I realize its importance. I rarely feel my heart beat and never the rush of blood through veins and arteries, yet let my heart begin to palpitate and in panic I know its importance; let a clot of my blood form and I may be too dead to know anything! My conscious motivations rule my life less than those hidden away in some submerged level of mind and heart that I may never know till judgment time. Who ever sees or hears the great God? TVs blast away, talk is about everything but him, thoughts and actions run contrary to him, and yet everything is only because of him. When he's unnoticed and unnoticeable in a crib in Bethlehem and on a cross on Calvary, in the horror and ugliness as well as the joy and beauty of the world, why shouldn't he be in what seems to be mere bread and wine?

These thoughts come to me when I'm tempted to disown the eucharist because of its fragility and the often sacrilegious celebration and reception of it. How fine when the eucharist is celebrated in a faith community with beautiful word and song! But when it's otherwise I must try to think of Calvary itself, which the eucharist *is*. That was, and is, no beautiful affair. Yet there is, and most intensely, my Lord and my God.

What a marvelous invention the eucharist is, Lord! It could have been dreamed up only by you — passionately in love with each and every human being from the beginning of time till now and beyond. "Having loved those who were his in the world, he loved them to the end" (Jn 13:1). There you were, Jesus, as your death was approaching, trying to figure out how you might remain with your friends — and remain most intimately and creatively not only with each one of them but with all of us. And the inspiration comes: "Give yourself to them as food and drink so that they might *become* you and you them. You will be not just outside but within them. It is for this that your love — that any true love — longs."

Now you come to me from within and direct my thought and love inward, in search not so much of an object to be known and loved but — as is the way of faith, that knowledge of the heart — of a subject that is knowing and loving. Your eucharistic presence within me feeds and nourishes my faculties, transforms them so that, more and more, inward awareness becomes sight of the same presence in the exterior world. St. Paul put it most simply: "Yet I live, no longer I, but Christ lives in me" (Gal 2:20). You live within me, so I see with your mind and love with your heart. I see not just the surface of things and people but into their depth, wherein you are lodged, deep calling unto deep. You, my Christ, become all in all. Yes, "in the end there will be one Christ in love with himself."

But I'm so far from home. I wonder why. For over half a century I've taken you upon my lips and into my heart, and for over half of that I've daily celebrated your eucharistic presence. Being so close to holiness all these years you'd think some of it would have rubbed off on me. By now I should be able to say and mean what Paul said and meant. Maybe, though, in some strange way I am holy but, like the rest of the insides of Christianity, I just can't see it. But what's the difference, really, what I see and feel? It's your sight that counts. In spite of all, I hope you see what pleases you.

Not long ago few Catholics would have thought to receive communion without first having confessed their sins to the priest and asked absolution of him. Such a practice was repugnant to Protestants, who regarded *any* practice involving a sacramental confession as heretical. Now Catholics themselves, whatever they might believe in theory about confession, in practice are protestant. Although they speak of it now less stringently as reconciliation, frequent reception of the sacrament is becoming more and more rare, not just among the laity but among priests and religious who profess to regret its loss.

There are many reasons for such a dramatic change in attitude. There's our current emphasis upon the mercy of God rather than on his justice and judgment and the corresponding belief that all such a merciful God requires for forgiveness is an act of sorrow and the resolve to do better. There's the preachment of other sources of forgiveness such as the Mass and works of charity and justice. There's the past abuse of the sacrament by those who, having nothing serious to confess, yet feeling they must receive the sacrament, would invent sins. There's the scrupulosity that the sacrament sometimes created or at least encouraged by requiring detailed confessions. There was the embarrassment of having to confess one's sexual sins, in kind and number, with resulting lies for coverup; and, as in the case of contraception, there was the demand to confess what one was not at all sure was sinful. There was sometimes the failure of the confessor to understand and empathize with human weakness. To top it all off, there was the grand exodus from the priesthood — an exodus that likely isn't at all over. The priest had once been regarded as a man apart who could and must keep secrets. What assures such privacy now that priests and former priests are "just like the rest of us"?

However grave such criticisms may be I find that I'm still glad the sacrament, by whatever name it may be called, is still around. For years I've seen it at work in my own life and in the lives of others. I've heard of damage done by it, but, for the most part, have experienced and witnessed its benefits. If in some cases scrupulosity and guilt have resulted from too frequent and indiscriminate use of the sacrament, from what I read and observe far greater evils result from its absence: One's sins and crimes remain locked within, sink into one's unconscious, decay and fester, and errupt in even more serious destructive behavior. With the confessional out of style the psychiatrist's office is all that's left — for those, that is, who can afford it.

I like the name "reconciliation," because this specifies the sacrament as a whole better than "confession," which is meant to be but one aspect of it. It designates the end or goal of the sacrament whereas confession speaks only of one of the means. The need for large-scale reconciliation — among nations, churches, religions, among and within families — is obvious. But it must begin with me, or at least involve me from the beginning. Personal reconciliation without social may be difficult to have and to hold, but social reconciliation without personal is simply a delusion.

But what does the traditional sacrament have to do with this personal reconciliation? Much, I think, providing we see and use it not as sometimes preached and practiced in the past but as it stands in the purity of the church's tradition. That tradition tells us first that the moment we say and mean we're sorry we're forgiven. Jesus' words, especially his parables, are clear on this. The prodigal son scarcely gets one word of repentence out before his father silences him with total forgiveness. The woman who anoints Jesus' feet says nothing but is immediately forgiven, for "she has loved much." Jesus demands that we forgive others not "seven times" but "seventy times seven," that is, with no limit, suggesting the readiness of God's own absolute forgiveness at all times.

But out of Jesus' words, "Whose sins you shall forgive they are forgiven . . . ," the church early evolved a *sacrament* of forgiveness. This highlighted both the need and the dignity of reconciliation and assured the special help of God in securing it. The church also gradually formulated a ritual emphasizing the sacred character of reconciliation and making it genuine and complete. The ritual embraced an examination of conscience, true sorrow, confession and absolution, and penance or reparation.

We must begin with an examination of conscience. Socrates had said that the unexamined life isn't worth living. Instead of ignoring our internal and external failures and thereby suffering them to sink underground and return to haunt us and others in crazy, harmful ways, it is better to face and face up to them. If we are ever to know our strengths we had better recognize our weaknesses. Knowing the enemy we've a better shot at victory. But the examination should also involve a recognition of our virtues and a thankful heart for all the goodness in our lives. Indeed, this should be considered first. I suspect the sin most committed and least confessed is that of ingratitude. Our examination of conscience should help us avoid this.

True sorrow doesn't mean tears and a long, unhappy face. It means regret for having thought or done a mean deed or failed to do a right one when called for. It entails a firm purpose to do right by God and neighbor in the future. Without such regret for misdeeds and purpose of amendment no reconciliation is possible, neither among nations, within familes, nor in our personal lives. If I'm to be your friend again after having slandered you I must apologize, try to rectify the damage done, and resolve never to do the like again. Otherwise we can only remain enemies with the sin always on, or worse below, my conscience.

Yes, the moment I say to God, and mean, that I'm sorry, I'm thereby forgiven. But confession of sin to another human being, preferably a priest who is bound *absolutely* to secrecy, is needed, for several reasons. First, it helps keep us honest: Self-deception is less likely when we have to verbalize our failures before another person. Second, to relieve an anxious conscience and alleviate psychological distress: It is always healthy and good to have a confidant, especially one whose job is to listen, and listen sympathetically and creatively. Third, for advice and counsel and encouragement, which may help bring us closer to God and not simply further from sin. Fourth, that we might ask pardon not just of God but of others whom we've offended. This is especially needed when, because of death or some other circumstance, someone we've harmed is now beyond our reach. The priest or minister may stand in that person's place, visibly receive our sorrow, and channel into our hearts the forgiveness that we long for. Fifth, and most important, absolution visibly brings us the fullness of *God's* forgiveness. The priest is not primarily a psychologist, counsellor, or comforter. He may be these also, but in the confessional, as at the eucharist and other sacraments, he is mainly and often exclusively the channel of Christ's forgiveness. It would be well for the priest to consider his lowly position when ministering the sacrament. Let him be silent and sparing of reproach and advice as much as possible that Christ might be heard and felt. In this as in other matters he should imitate the Lord, who had little enough to say when he forgave sins: "Has no one condemned you?" . . . "No one, sir" . . . "Neither do I condemn you . . . . Go away, and from this moment sin no more" (Jn 8:10–11).

Penance or reparation, the final requirement of reconciliation, is not exclusive to Christianity. The orientals speak of "karma," of some sort of "righting of the balance," a making good, now or in another life, of something that was bad. Rightly considered, the church's demand for reparation or penance has similar roots. It's not that I must suffer now, be punished, because I did something wrong. Rather, having done something wrong, I must now make it right, though in doing so I may have to suffer. The priest must be mindful of this, and make sure the penitent is mindful of it, when he "assigns a penance." He is demanding of me, the sinner, what I myself, if truly sorrowful, want — the righting of the wrong I have done. He may ask me to fast, or he may assign certain prayers or works of charity or justice as penance, but these are merely gestures in the direction of reparation. If I have been angry my real penance is undoing the harm my anger has caused and, probably at grave inconvenience, even downright suffering, avoiding anger in the future. If I have committed sins of lust I must truly *love* now, especially those whom I've demeaned. If I have been slothful I must now begin to *do* for God and his kingdom, to be part of the solution and not of the problem. Again, Jesus, with the woman caught in adultery: He assigns her no penance except that of committing this sin no more — a big job for her, perhaps, and a painful one, but not a punishment. It is simply the way now of love, which genuine sorrow itself demands.

Nothing of this, of course, should be forced on people. The sacrament should be preached and ministered in the manner of Jesus — as invitation, not as demand. Priests, especially, should begin again to value the sacrament for themselves and, by prayer, study, and the practice of compassion, prepare for ministering it to others. As with the eucharist, so much depends upon the minister's desire to empty himself and let Christ and *his* loving mercy and forgiveness shine through.

As always, Lord, though we aim for the ideal we must not be too disappointed when things fall short of it. We can only go limping and stumbling along, making our usual mess of things. But you make up the difference. Here's another fine thing about this sacrament of yours: It works in and through us but also beyond us. We make our feeble, awkward gesture of sorrow and repentance and you graciously sweep us up into your healing love — so eager are you to forgive and forget.

The eucharist is the body and blood of Christ. It's also his spoken word. That first eucharist, especially as John recounts it, was filled with the precious words of Jesus — a sermon greater than that on the Mount, one that asks of us the best we have and more and makes it all sound real, attainable, desirable: "Love one another as I have loved you" (Jn 15:12). In every eucharist since, the word of Christ precedes and surrounds the making of his body to prepare us for it and deepen it within us. The eucharist, then, is the origin and the fulfillment of Christian preaching. It is the pattern of all Christian preaching — not my word but Christ's, and Christ's word as leading to the most intimate personal and communal union with him.

Always in the best tradition of the church the liturgy of the word and the liturgy of the body are hand in glove. One or other may be neglected in practice — in the Catholic church it has been the preaching, while in Protestant churches by and large it has been the liturgy of the body — but this does not negate the doctrine. Rather, the doctrine judges and condemns failures in practice.

Thus, while repeating the traditional teaching that the principal act of the priest is the celebration of the eucharist, the Second Vatican Council declared and stressed that his "primary duty" is to proclaim the gospel. The council also set the stage for the laity, both men and women, to enter into this work. Since the council, and on the strength of it, emphasis has been placed not just upon reading the scriptures but upon their prayerful and scientific *study*, that the gospel might be learned, and spoken, truly.

But precisely because scriptural science has advanced so rapidly and so far within the church in the course of the last half century, preaching the gospel is becoming more and more problematic. Disciplines meant to grow together in mutual support and nourishment seem to be growing apart. I'm not thinking simply of critical historical exegesis vis-a-vis fundamentalist preaching, though here the problem is large and obvious. I'm thinking of preachers — myself included — who respect and value and even teach the discoveries and interpretations of much of contemporary hermeneutics and, equally, want to preach Jesus to a world desperately in need of him. For if I am to preach Jesus as he objectively was and is and not just my subjective idea and experience of him, where am I to find him?

At one time the answer was obvious enough. Initially, Jesus could be found in the gospels as a long and blessed tradition has preserved and interpreted them for us, and then, with this as ground, in our communal and individual experience of him. Now, however, the "ground" has been radically disturbed. Jesus, along with the rest of religious belief and practice, has been increasingly subjectivized. From a Sweitzer to a Fiorenza, from a LaGrange to a Raymond Brown, the alteration in the reading of the gospel has been a gradual but dramatic one. Whereas formerly the gospels were regarded mainly as the inspired history of Jesus, relating words and deeds he physically spoke and did, now they are seen as theological tracts presenting not the historical Jesus but the early church's interpretation of him. As the chairman of the "Jesus Seminar" is reported to have said of John's gospel: "Jesus of the gospel of John is a figment of the evangelist's pious imagination." If we want to find the real Jesus we must look not *in* the gospels but *behind* them. In this attempt to get behind the gospels to the true Jesus a growing minority find the gospels more of an obstacle than an aid: Rather than a true picture of Jesus they present us with the early church's myopic, often distorted, view of him.

In addition it's considered uncritical to speak of the "early church," as though there was but one church in the beginning, as traditionally believed. Actually, there were many early churches: that of Mark, Matthew, Luke, John, Paul, James. The divisions and conflicts within these churches are emphasized and almost exclusively dwelled upon. The early heretical sects, now more and more appreciated as "churches," are added to them as part of the competing menagerie, just as the apocryphal gospels are placed side by side with the canonical and treated with equal, sometimes greater respect.

Further, the gospels are no longer seen *together* as a whole with each of them contributing its nuance or addition to the totality of the life of Jesus. Rather than adding up to a single story with at least some semblance of a chronology, they are mere fragments of a life (if that!) often at odds with each other, and having nothing at all to do with "chronology." In times past the differences were appreciated and the uniqueness of each gospel recognized, as in the liturgy's proclamation: "A reading from the holy gospel according to Mark . . . Luke . . . John . . ." But mere difference has now become absolute diversity. If not yet in the pulpit then certainly in the classroom it is each of the gospels and fragments of each that must be specified. One can no longer gather the four gospels together, much less the rest of the New Testament, and refer to them simply as "the gospel of Jesus Christ." *That* gospel, together with the life it proclaims, has yet to be discovered or, in the parlance of the professionals, "reconstructed."

In view of this revolution in scriptural studies what are preachers to do? They may, as many do, preach only their own experience or some exegete's construction of Jesus, though they may feel nervous about having no objective, communal ground for such preachment. Or, as do the fundamentalists, they may ignore the whole contemporary hermeneutical thing and cleave to the traditional (as they see it) way of reading the scriptures. But there's another way, somewhere in the middle, which is closer to, or at least less distant from, the truth.

First, it is Jesus who is to be preached, and Jesus not as behind the gospels but within them as witnessed to by those first Christian preachers from Mary Magdalene to the last of the apostles. Jesus as the gospels present him *is* the historical Jesus. If "historical" means only the external words and deeds of a person then, yes, there may be little of the history of

Jesus within the gospels; though we may suspect that much
of what so great and loving a person physically said and did
was deeply graved on the memories of his disciples and would
be proclaimed by them. But one's history is much more than
this. It's what underlies the visible deed and audible word —
the spirit of a person that often can be detected only by the
Spirit.

> Thoughts hardly to be packed
> Into a narrow act,
> Fancies that broke through language and escaped;
> All I could never be,
> All men ignored in me,
> This I was worth to God, whose wheel the
> pitcher shaped.

As Browning's verse suggests, Jesus' history was mainly
what filled his words and deeds and broke out of them into
a marvelous fullness that only his Holy Spirit could grasp
and then, by way of inspiration, relate to the rest of us. Does
it really concern me, then, if, for instance, Jesus physically,
audibly spoke only one or two of the beatitudes instead of the
four mentioned by Luke or the eight mentioned by Matthew?
Need I say it was all word for word as Jesus preached it, or
may I not, with Vatican II, look upon the gospels as selection
and synthesis as well as record of Jesus' life? Those words
and deeds omitted by one or other or all of the evangelists
are implied in what is actually recorded. And if they did not
issue from Jesus' tongue they did from his Spirit, as his Spirit
inspired the early church to preach and write them down. In
either case it is Jesus, the historically *complete* Jesus, who
spoke and did all that the gospels relate of him.

Of course, one can deny the Spirit's inspiration of the
gospels and so treat them simply as secular history. But if
this is so then the gospels are not unique literature nor is

Jesus much more than a question mark. Why spend so much time and effort searching common ordinary documents for one whose worth is dubious at best? At any rate, we end up not with an historical person but with the "pious imagination" (to use the Jesus' seminar's phrase in another direction) of exegetical and theological speculators.

Second, because of this fullness of the historical Jesus given us by the Spirit, we have several gospels. They may contradict each other on various visible and audible "facts" about Jesus, they may differ in chronology, but, as argued above, these are only the surface of history. What they do agree upon is the spirit, the life, underlying the so-called facts. Each of the gospels explores this in its unique way out of its own time and circumstances, adding to our appreciation of the magnitude of Jesus' life and encouraging us to view that life from the perspective of our own time and circumstances, to truly make the *one* gospel of Jesus a never-ending affair. If we credit each of the gospels with a special providence in its construction and preservation can we not also see a like providence in bringing them, and only them, together into a single book with a unified story and message? If we expect only diversity this is all we shall find. But if we are alert for an underlying unity we shall find this as well.

Third, in this fullness of Jesus the early churches were radically the *one* church of Christ. Like the gospels that issued from them, they differed in their emphases on one or another aspect of Jesus but overall it was, as Paul witnessed, "one Lord, one faith, one baptism" (Eph 4:5). The felt need for unity was intense; thus from earliest times the dread of heresy and schism and the cry for one flock under one shepherd were present. The differences among the several churches may have been profound and blatant, but deeper still, as evidenced from the whole of the New Testament and the theology of the churches of the first several centuries, was oneness in the life, death, and resurrection of Jesus the Lord. This early pattern also seems providential, inviting, exhorting us to look for similar diversity with essential, substantive unity at its heart among the contemporary Christian churches.

Without surrendering then to the verbal absurdities of an entrenched fundamentalism or the tenuous subtleties of an exaggerated hermeneutics, I try to preach Jesus as revealed within the gospel, that is, the whole of the New Testament. I feel free to move from one gospel to another in the same sermon, choosing incidents and sayings of Jesus with respect for their individual contexts, of course, but also for the wholeness of the revealed narrative that bears the unity as well as diversity of the Spirit's inspiration. I preach the annunciation and the visitation that follows it; I don't know the exact words spoken or heard but I believe that the words written express, as nearly as possible, the "historical" words *within the heart* of the angel, Mary, Elizabeth. I preach the birth of Jesus, feeling free to move from Luke to Matthew and back again, as, evidently, the inspiring, all-encompassing Spirit felt free to do initially. Again, I don't know the perceptible details of what was said and done but I believe it was infinitely more marvelous than related, and what in fact *is* related is calculated by the Spirit to bring me deep into these marvels of *history*. The same holds true for Jesus' prayer, his revolutionary words and deeds, his compassion, his healing ministry, his miracles.

Yes, his miracles too, not as accentuating his divinity at the expense of his humanity but as proving the potential of the human when rightly centered. Here is the message of the *historical* Jesus. The suffering and death, the empty tomb and the resurrected Christ, are all to be preached as found within the four gospels, singly and together, and in the rest of the New Testament. Again, the narration as given by the Spirit and received by the evangelists is sparse, often obscure, sometimes self-contradictory, especially as it concerns those tense, vibrant, meaningful times of suffering, death, and resurrection. Such strained and elevated moments are bound to mystify and confuse. So much was happening in so brief a time — much more *history* than could possibly be recorded.

We owe a great debt to contemporary scriptural science, and some of the best of our exegetes and biblical theologians would, I think, be close to one mind with me in the concerns if not in the solution offered here. But by and large in scriptural studies today there's a minimalist mentality. The question seems to be: What is the very least we can say about the authentic, historical Jesus? The answer often suggests that the least is the most that can be said. But the gospels together with the tradition that birthed and followed them are for maximalization. Again, this is why we have four gospels and Paul and the other canonical writers contemplating a history instead of just one gospel neatly constructing and packaging mere myth. Jesus said at the Last Supper: "When the Paraclete comes, whom I shall send to you from the Father, the Spirit of truth who issues from the Father, he will be my witness. . . . When the Spirit of truth comes, he will lead you to the complete truth" (Jn 15:26; 16:13). And at the very end of the four gospels we are told: "There was much else that Jesus did; if it were written down in detail, I do not suppose the world itself would hold all the books that would be written" (Jn 21:25).

As many today insist, Jesus himself, not the documents that proclaim him, *is* the gospel, the good news. Granted. But the Word is to be found within the words that the Spirit uttered in and through those first preachers of the nascent church. These words are the sine qua non, the very sacrament, of the presence of Jesus among us. They reveal to us Jesus as he was two thousand years ago, as he is now, and as he will be in the future. It's these words, then, that the preacher must reverence, study, and pray over in order to preach them, and so Jesus, to the world of our time.

SEVEN

Ministry
of the Word

Preaching is (should be) the work, the ongoing work, of the Holy Spirit. This is true of any creative work: "Only the Spirit if He breathe upon the clay can create man." But it's especially true of preaching. In the beginning the Spirit of God hovered over the chaotic waters as God *said*, "Let there be light...": first the Spirit and then out of the Spirit the word and light. It was the same at the beginning of the second creation: Out of the Spirit's "coming upon" Mary, the living Word of God, the Light of the world, was conceived. The same for the third creation: the Holy Spirit hovered over the nascent church in tongues of fire, and the preaching began.

This makes good sense. If I'm to preach I'm to preach Christ. But if I'm to preach Christ I've got to know him. But how know him except in and through his Spirit? "When the Spirit of truth comes, he will lead you to the complete truth...He will glorify me, since all he reveals to you will be taken from what is mine" (Jn 16:13–14). Only the Spirit, with Mary, can bring Christ to birth in the minds and hearts of those to whom I preach. Too big a job for me alone! Therefore I'm not to *force* my words on another or think too much of my part in the preaching. I'm to leave room for the Spirit to enter into my words and get between them and so speak to the individual heart beyond them.

Preaching should be properly motivated. This may seem obvious, but the obvious is most often forgotten or ignored. False or less worthy motives keep intruding. We ought to recognize and be alert for them and take due action against them. There's the profit motive. Sometimes it's crass enough to be readily detected, as when I find myself personally becoming rich or at least materially comfortable because of my preaching. But often the snake is well hidden in the grass. I may not, for instance, preach to fill my own pocket, but in order that I might benefit a worthy cause — the missions, homeless children, education of seminarians, the relief of one disease or another. Fine as a by-product of the preaching — maybe; but only if it is truly "aside" or happens to be one with the very message of Christ being preached at the moment. And I must make sure that whatever money comes from the preaching doesn't stop short with me but gets to the poor, in one way or another. Also I must beware of feelings of elation when the collection is up and discouragement when it's down, of rendering services when the price is right and withholding them when it's not.

There's the pleasure motive: I preach because I like to preach, much as an actor on stage. If I'm good at preaching most likely I'll get pleasure out of it, and certainly I *should* be pleased when I see it bearing fruit for Christ. But again, this should be a by-product, not my goal. I'm to preach even when it's painful and when no good results are apparent...even should it mean crucifixion while and after I preach, as it did for the Lord himself and for many a devoted preacher since.

There's the motive of pride: If the sermon's good my self-esteem receives a boost. People admire me and I like that. This is especially dangerous, since *I* then, not Christ, become the center of my preaching. And because it's all done in the name of holiness we end up thinking that this is the way it should be. Christ has been quietly put aside and there is ridiculous little old me in his place.

There's the motive of power. Yes, religion is a tremendous force, an instinct within us stronger than any other. If I can control or manipulate it people can be made slaves to my will and, like the Jim Joneses of the world, I can make or break them. This can be a great and subtle temptation for certain preachers of talent and charisma. For obvious reasons the temptation is to be recognized and resisted, even, if need be, to the point of surrendering one's preaching mission altogether.

"This is the greatest treason, to do the right deed for the wrong reason." Wisdom worth pondering by one who would be *Christ's* preacher.

The proper motivation for preaching is the building up of the body of Christ. But what specifically does this mean? Quite simply, it means that I am to aim at bringing people closer to God. What people?

I'm to preach to those of other faiths or no faith at all, the modern counterpart of the ancient gentile. This was Christianity's original thrust: Jesus' command to go out to all nations; and Paul's and the other disciples' mission to the gentiles. Christianity's preaching, unlike that of other religions, has been *missionary* from the beginning to the present day. This is a big job, one many claim is impossible and even undesirable. We must continually develop ways of reaching the "gentile" through the kind of preaching — humble, respectful, reverent — that finds as well as brings Christ where *apparently* he is not.

Here is where the fostering, educating, and commissioning of lay preachers seems most urgent: deacons, deaconesses, and other ministers, not to crowd and clutter the altar at Sunday liturgies but for the secular world in which they live and work. They are to preach not from the pulpit but on the job, in the media, in the home, on the streets, and in ways attractive to the variety of congregations to be found "out there." Priest preachers are no longer enough, nor have been for a very long time. If preaching to the gentiles is to continue, or rather begin again, it must be in and through committed laity. Fairly obvious? But how little is being done, or will be done, about it!

The main work of clergy like myself lies in preaching to the "ordinary" Catholic within the church building at regular liturgical worship. This is not to be slighted or lamented as being ingrown: "saving the saved" as it used to be said. A good preacher with a well-prepared and prayed over sermon on a Sunday or holyday or at another opportune time can do much to awaken the faithful to a new appreciation of their faith, and maybe even inspire some of them to become preachers themselves. There are also at such services the *anawim*, God's little ones who hunger and thirst for holiness but find little to feed them. They've had milk long enough, they now require meat. Preaching that will touch their minds and hearts, help them to persevere in prayer and continually deepen it, inspire them to works of charity and justice is also "missionary" preaching: The mission of the church is not just to convert the unbeliever and save sinners, but to make holy. Jesus reached out to all but he did not neglect his special friends, his regular congregation; indeed, he spent most of his time and energy for them.

Preaching and teaching are or can be one and the same. The irony is that many of those most vocal about their right to preach from the pulpit are those who have given up on teaching. What a loss to the church that so many gifted teachers have sought employment elsewhere, while others of us have seriously compromised Christian teaching and radically secularized it. But what a *preaching* apostolate for the laity! What better way to reach the atheist, the agnostic, the non-Christian, the alienated Christian than through serious research and publication, and through ideas proposed, discussed, argued in the classroom where young and not so young are in search of meaning and will carry out into the secular world the truths they've gathered?

Ideas more than deeds, quiet thought more than social action and protest, change the world. Think of a Buddha, a Confucius, think of Jesus and his revolutionary *ideas*. Think of Freud, Darwin, Marx, Pierre and Marie Curie, Einstein. Who has done more to revolutionize our present world than such men and women of ideas, research, and quiet communication? Think of Bach, Mozart, Beethoven, of Michelangelo, Van-Gogh, Picasso, of Dante, Shakespeare, Eliot. Who has done more for culture and cultural changes than these *contemplatives* and specialists in the "word"?

Here are the real leaders, the "movers and shakers of the world," not those with elected or usurped power, magnates of authority in Church and State. Government and politics, yes; private and social action, yes. But the thought and the word, whether of sound or color, underlie and inspire the politics and the deed. Here the revolutions begin and often culminate, whatever the mindless proponents of pragmatic action, the quick fix, the existential moment, shout to the contrary.

Prayer is of the essence of right preaching, the kind that is of both head and heart, involving both prayer and prayerful study. The prayer of asking, certainly: We ask that we might be worthy and effective preachers of God's word; we pray for inspiration for a given sermon and the energy to think it through; and we pray for those to whom we'll be preaching. But more important than petition is contemplative prayer, wherein we empty ourselves of our own thoughts and ideas of God that we might be filled with what God wants us to think and speak. Through such prayer we come to know God, not just ideas of God, and it is God — not our ideas of him — that we are to preach. This preparatory contemplative prayer of mine goes beyond preparation to enter into the formulation of my sermon and the actual preaching of it. It precedes the sermon but it also accompanies and follows it, as life does action.

My own contemplative prayer, however, is not enough for my preaching, because I'm not good enough at it. And so I seek out the "professionals," those who have dedicated their lives to contemplation, the Carmelites, for instance, or my Dominican cloistered sisters and others whom I know and respect as contemplatives. I try consciously and prayerfully to root all my preaching and writing in the depth of their prayer. The deeper my sermon is grounded in prayer the higher and further will it extend. I look, then, to the deepest contemplation that I know and let my preaching grow out of that.

A further reason why I must be contemplatively prayerful is that one of the most urgent needs my preaching can un- cover and satisfy is the need to pray, and pray meditatively, contemplatively. If I can bring people into the *real presence*, the *shekina* of God, if, that is, I can teach them to pray, what more need I do for them? The Spirit herself will do the rest. But how can I teach others to pray when I can't or don't?

Experience is also essential to preaching. If it is to be real and vital, preaching must grow out of the lives and faith of the people to whom we preach. If we don't think and feel with the people we can't preach to them. Some young dons of the University of Cambridge were singing the praises of the Ivy League universities they had just visited. An old retired professor was listening intently but when the eulogizing was over his only comment was a question: "Yes, but do they dine together?" Scholarship must be communal, rooted in common day-to-day living, talking, working, dining *together*. This is especially true of the highest form of scholarship, theology. It's the same, then, with preaching, which is the heartfelt expression of a prayerful theology. We preach Christ; therefore we must live with Christ who abides with and in those to whom we preach.

But more is needed than raw experience. The dull of mind and heart may have many experiences with little if any profit for anyone, while for those alert and sensitive, out of a single experience comes a wealth of meaning. *Reflective* experience is required, and prayerful experience, that is, experience from above as well as from below. Otherwise we make of our own little world the whole world. We lose the *catholic* perspective and so contribute to, rather than remedy, the fragmentation and diminution of Christ.

Preaching and teaching were Jesus' prime vocation and became that of Paul and the other apostles. Jesus fed and healed bodies but much more to his purpose was the feeding and healing of minds and spirits. "Not on bread alone . . ." For Jesus, body, mind, and spirit were one, and you don't really heal one without effective concern for the others. But the healing of mind and spirit through teaching and preaching was the more radical and necessary for Jesus and his apostles. It should be the same for us.

Independently of Jesus' example we can see that the world is most in need of good Christian preaching and teaching, that is, the communication of the fullness of truth personalized in Jesus Christ. Aristotle said that you can't philosophize on an empty stomach. Difficult to theologize on an empty stomach, too, or to hear and respect the words of the preacher. Feeding the hungry, giving drink to the thirsty, and so on have their priorities, but the minds and spirits of the poor are hungry too. To be concerned only or even mainly for their bodies is to violate their dignity and to prolong their poverty. But

to educate them in the truth and wisdom of Christ, which
involves both secular and sacred learning, is to give them the
wherewithal to fight their own battles for justice, to live at
least moderately happy lives, and be creative in the lives of
others. The rich, too — in some ways even more than the
poor — require that the word of God be preached and taught
to them, that in their discovery or rediscovery of God they
might realize they are stewards not possessors of the world's
wealth and that their greatest happiness lies in service and in
giving.

The old cliche, "Those who can, do, those who can't,
teach," ought to be recognized for what it is: excrement!
Teaching, as preaching, *is* doing, and the highest form of doing. It's action of the most intense kind, and productive of
other forms of meaningful action, as should be evident to all
who have eyes to see and ears to hear. The same goes for the
intellectual and prayerful life that is its grounding. It is truly
life out of which other life results. Dedicated teachers and
preachers, researchers, scholars, writers, artists, musicians, poets, contemplative monks and nuns, need not apologize for
their vocation, for their only critics are those who don't know
how to live and, except for the happy chance of some inspired
preacher or teacher coming their way, never will.

EIGHT

Ways of Love

Once upon a time the church distinguished three states of life — marriage, widowhood, and celibacy — and ranked them, in the order here listed, as good, better, and best. Celibacy and widowhood were given the edge over marriage, not because of what was surrendered — human, sexual love — but because of what was aimed at — the perfect love of God. "The unmarried woman [widow?]," said St. Paul, "and the virgin, gives her mind to the Lord's affairs and to being holy in body and spirit" (1 Cor 7:34). Although, like St. Paul, they counseled virginity, the early Apostolic Canons warned: "If any bishop or priest or deacon or, indeed, anyone from the body of clerics, abstains from marriage, meat and wine, not from the motive of mortification, but because of detestation for them, forgetful that all things are exceedingly good and that God made man male and female; but blaspheming, finds fault with creation, let him either be corrected, or deposed and cast out of the Church." The fourth century Council of Gangra was equally clear and firm as to what the motive of celibacy must and must not be:

> If anyone despises wedlock, abhoring and blaming the woman who sleeps with her husband, even if she is a believer and devout, as if she could not enter the kingdom of God, let him be anathema. . . . If anyone lives unmarried or in continence, avoiding marriage from contempt, and not because of the beauty and holiness of virginity,

137

let him be anathema. . . . If anyone of those who for the Lord's sake remain single, in pride exalts himself above those who are married, let him be anathema. . . . If a woman leaves her husband and separates herself, from an abhorrence of the marriage state, let her be anathema.

The great medieval theologians likewise qualified their recommendation of celibacy. St. Thomas, for instance, when treating of the worth of celibacy doesn't speak simply of virginity but of "devoted, directed" virginity (*pia virginitas*), virginity that "allows greater liberty for contemplation and divine service." Those, he says, who are celibate because of a detestation of sex and marriage are warped by the vice of insensibility (*insensibilitas*): They are "boorishly without feeling" (*insensibilis quasi agrestis*). Whatever the divergencies of particular theologians and preachers, this authoritative teaching was made clear enough to the average layperson of the time. "Chastity without charity is chained in hell," wrote William Langland in the most popular and dogmatically conservative of the late medieval English "epics." Celibacy, as a call to perfect charity, might have more going for it than the vocation of marriage, but it was commonly recognized that many a spouse might be nearer the Lord than many a virgin. Then, as now, it was what you did in and with your particular vocation that counted.

I should think it would have been difficult, if not impossible, for the medieval church not to see and preach the higher worth of celibacy. Granted, as some argue, celibacy was to its material advantage: Clergy, having no family as heirs, must leave their holdings to the church. But long before this idea would have suggested itself, the example of Christ and Paul had its influence. If Christ and his greatest disciple were celibate and, according to the exegesis of the time, had recommended celibacy, then celibacy must be of considerable worth, something to be prized even above marriage. And it must be promoted more than marriage since marriage, being natural, we simply fall into, whereas celibacy, being beyond nature, we must reach for and be raised to.

Another, perhaps more basic reason, why celibacy was so esteemed was the sense of the transitoriness of this life and the imminent advent of God's kingdom where "they neither marry nor are given in marriage" (Mt 22:30, *NAB*). Apparently, the earliest Christians were convinced that Christ in his glory would "come quickly," but even as this conviction dimmed in the realization that life as we know it now would continue, still, as St. Paul emphasized, here we are pilgrims only, and we must continually be reminded of the fact and prodded forward. What better reminder of this than celibacy? Marriage not only immerses one in this material world but, through the propagation of children, also adds to it and contributes toward its continuation. Thus the need for some not simply to preach the limitation and end of this world but in their very persons to draw apart from it in radical ways so as to shock others into the consideration that there may be something more.

There was also in the past church as in the present the fervent desire on the part of some for total commitment to God. But it was difficult in former times to see how *ordinarily* one could be totally committed to God while absorbed in marriage and the affairs of the world that marriage involves one in. Earlier Christians believed in Christ and the *body* of Christ and so the body of the world and the marriage bond that affirmed it. But the best part of Christ's body was the access it provided to his divinity. The visible world was good, the visible Christ was holy, but best of all was the invisible God, and celibacy best enabled one to reach for and rest in him.

Such thinking is still alive in the church, although, it would seem, barely so. The worth of celibacy has been seriously and widely challenged twice in the history of the western church: at the time of the Reformation by what came to be known as Protestantism, and now among those who are and, in good conscience, intend to remain Roman Catholics. The arguments offered are formidable.

First, marriage extols and celebrates the worth of creation and of the creator God. Whereas celibacy draws us apart from the world, marriage involves us in it. It makes of us partners with God in his very act of creation, by begetting children, certainly, but also by begetting each other. It becomes the channel, the vehicle, and therefore the sign or sacrament of God's creative love for each of us. Celibacy may speak of God's love coming from afar. Marriage speaks of it as up close and operative in our day-to-day life. Further, the married, by loving each other and their children, and precisely by being involved in the affairs of the world, are thereby loving God himself, and loving him every bit as directly and intimately as the celibate: "When I was hungry you gave *me* to eat. . . . "

This conjugal love is intimate to a degree and in ways which are not possible in celibate love. In marriage two people can give themselves totally to each other and to their children, and total giving and receiving is of the nature of love — indeed, love at its best. But as a celibate, though I may long to give myself totally to another I must hold back, must do violence to love, and make sure the other does too. I may, through the freedom that celibacy provides, be able to love more people, but what I gain in breadth I lose in depth. So in the long run, what is the worth of celibacy over marriage? What, indeed, is the worth of celibacy at all?

But even granting that celibacy *in ideal* is supreme over marriage, in reality it fails, often drastically. In the tradition of much medieval satire Luther and the other reformers raged against monkish and priestly sexual degeneracy. In our own day the exodus from clerical and religious life testifies to the ongoing failure of celibacy. And of those who continue to profess celibacy, how many are truly celibate? There are those who are secretly but blythly promiscuous, sometimes in terribly destructive ways. Others, while remaining superficially faithful, are unhappy, lonely, depressed over the thought that *never* will they have a full and intimate love of their own. Still others, whose appetite for human love has been suppressed, end up narcissists, alcoholics, old maids and bachelors. They fall into the vice of *insensibilitas* that Thomas Aquinas warned celibates against. In brief, celibacy is supposed to bring one out of self into the lives of others; instead it seems to suck one into oneself and foster the selfish life. What, then, becomes of the so-called symbolic value of celibacy? It would seem that instead of reminding people of the transcendent God and our need to reach beyond the transitoriness of this world into his everlastingness, celibacy rather distracts from God both beyond and within the world. Best, then, to do without it.

And, practically speaking, wouldn't it serve the church better if we let celibacy go in favor of a married clergy and ministry? The church is desperately in need of priestly ministry. Why, then, make that ministry dependent upon that which discourages many who otherwise would be glad to serve? And, since much of priestly ministry is to the married in their way of life, doesn't it seem obvious that a married clergy would be more effective? What do I, a celibate, know of the life and problems of the married? And if I'm thus ignorant, of what practical use am I?

Such have been the arguments against celibacy that have been forced upon me for many years now, and are daily voiced by scholarly journal as well as popular press, in stale repetition or fresh nuance. I'd like to offer a bit of rebuttal, not so much to deny as to fill in and round out the picture.

I don't think it's altogether fair to point to individual and even mass failures in the celibate life and thereby conclude that celibacy no longer has value. See the enormous failures in marriage, yet most of us by far still recognize and appreciate its worth. We do so because deep in our bones we know that it can be made to work and we find that often in fact it does work. I think it's the same with celibacy. As with marriage, we read and hear about its failures but, if we've the will to see, we witness its successes: men and women who are marvelously devoted to the Lord and his work and, in spite of their aloneness, at peace and often in joy. They may fail now and again in their vow as in other ways, but such it is to be a sinner, in constant need of healing and perfecting. And whatever failure may be there, there's success enough to give others pause and tease them into the consideration that, yes, the celibate may have a secret worth knowing.

It's scarcely beneficial to unearth the old question as to which is the greater, marriage or celibacy. Can't we simply say that each is necessary to and complementary of the other? In a purely secularized Christianity celibacy would have no place. Marriage and its symbolization of the holiness of the body of the world would be enough and celibacy not only superfluous but heretical. But secular Christianity is simply secularism in religious guise and as self-destructive as its original. The world is good and holy, but unless we reach beyond it to the transcendent God who makes it so, we mar and eventually destroy it. Here is one reason why the whole business of human sexuality is in such disarray. It's been made to stand on its own and become an ultimate: secular sex exclusive of the sacred. What's required is not simply a sermon on keeping love clean and whole and reaching beyond itself, but healthy human beings demonstrating by their very lives the possibility and urgency of transcendent love. What's needed, in other words, are *devoted* celibates. Let those married in the Lord be true to their vocation of blessing, sanctifying, expanding the world. But let there also be true celibates pointing to the source of all blessing and sanctification and directing the married to this underlying and overriding goal of all their striving.

It's true that the married enjoy an intimacy in love that is not possible for the celibate. But it's a sad and tragic fact that in most cases conjugal intimacy is of brief duration. Two strangers meet, get to know each other, love each other, and in virtue of that love find that they have become one in thought, desire, in body and in life, their own life and the life of the child birthed from such intimacy: the Trinity itself — Father, Child, and Mother Spirit — reflected as nearly as it can be in this world. But then come the inevitable separations: the misunderstandings, the *non*-understandings, the disagreements, the unexpected sicknesses, the losses, the deaths. What had been one has now become multiple, and the resulting loneliness is often far greater than that suffered by the celibate. A new union in love on a deeper level is possible, but only to the extent that the message written in the life of the celibate has been heard. The married must, as the celibate's life preaches, reach beyond and deep within themselves and their children to the God who stands above as well as within them and who alone can heal, secure, and perfect their love.

Also celibates can enjoy an intimacy in love in ways and to a degree that surpass that of the married. There's intimacy with God through loving contemplative prayer, often far more powerful in both spirit and flesh than that enjoyed/suffered by the most ardent of lovers. But there's also intimacy with others. Precisely because the celibate loves in ways other than sexual he becomes privy to secrets of the heart that are hidden from others and even from the self. I've found that as priest I've often known more about spouses and children of a given marriage than they knew of each other, and have sometimes entered into their lives more intimately than they themselves. This would raise little argument except that we've come to identify intimacy with sexual intimacy. The celibate having none of the latter is therefore thought to have no intimacy at all. This isn't a limitation of celibacy but of the way we think and feel in our time.

Which brings me to our final argument leveled against celibacy: the need for a married clergy. I must say amen to this. Not, however, for reasons frequently cited. Marriage alone is no remedy for unchaste clerics — all the failures in chastity found among celibates are there also, often in graver kind and larger numbers, among the married —and, as just argued, it is no escape from loneliness. Also, I, together with many of the married whom I know, don't at all buy the argument that a married clergy would better understand the problems of the married. Chances are the celibate is equally versed in them. The celibate was born into a family and grew up in it and, unless completely devoid of memory, knows in mind and bone both the joys and sorrows of family life. But also I've found that as a celibate priest I often know much more about marriage in general and about particular marriages than the married. A good part of my life I spend studying marriage, in books (often written by the married), in seminars (often conducted by the married), and in personal encounter with the married. I have also at times been able to relate to their children better than they and sometimes have been responsible for the reconciliation of children with parents, as well as of spouses with one another. I can, by my life and preaching, tell the married about dimensions in their marriage that they are ignorant of. . .just as they can remind me of things about my priesthood that I need to hear. As suggested above, the celibate can and should be a creative part of family life, just as the married should be part of the life of the celibate.

This said, I must add that the arguments against a married clergy seem to me as feeble as those for it but, in light of so grave a need, more reprehensible. Let there continue to be clergy who wish to remain celibate. They, if truly celibate, will, in general, have a fuller, richer ministry than married priests, having more time and freedom for prayer, study, service. But a well-trained, devoted married clergy will not only supplement desperately needed sacramental ministry but may in the long run prove to be efficacious in presently undreamed of ways. If it be argued that the abolition of the inflexibility of the rule of celibacy will result in the eventual demise of celibacy altogether, I should reply that such an attitude betrays a lack of faith in the power of celibacy and of the God who wants it. Those who are celibate simply because they're forced to be so are not truly celibate, so best, for themselves and the church at large, that they be free to marry. Otherwise they will end up *insensibilis* — self-centered and selfish. They become destroyers rather than promoters of God and his kingdom. Those who are truly and happily celibate will continue to be a sign of the presence of the transcendent God and will attract others freely and gladly to adopt their style of life. Who knows, maybe this line of action is precisely what's needed to restore celibacy to its intended dignity. It may even make it popular!

But celibacy to be such must be true. This means primarily that it must be positive. It must be an act of love. I think it has been this for many, but if language betrays thought and feeling one would suspect the opposite. Ask the question, even of a celibate, as to what a celibate is, chances are you'll get the response: It's someone who vows not to marry. It's not simply the uninitiate who respond so; it's the message of current ecclesiastical practice. Thus a priest who asks to be dispensed from his ministry is dispensed of all but his vow of celibacy. He can do everything now that a lay person can except marry. The restriction is even more pronounced when the priest is a religious. He will be dispensed from his vow of obedience, his vow of poverty — he may now be as independent as he likes and as rich as he likes and violate no ecclesiastical law. But he is still bound, and for life, to his vow of celibacy, which doesn't mean that by ecclesiastical law he is to continue to love, but simply that he can never marry.

Such an attitude is false, scandalous, contrary to the initial teaching of the church, and destructive of the lives of many who, having failed in one way of life, ask the merciful Lord for a chance at another in which they might continue to serve,

if not still as priests then in some other form of ministry, and
be blessed rather than condemned for doing so. Celibacy, if it
is to endure, must be thought of less and less as a prohibition
against marrying and more and more as a commitment to love:
to love God in and through deep and vital prayer, and others
through caring service. It is not failure in sexual behavior
that is the prime violation of celibacy. Rather it is a failure to
pray, long and deeply, and to be a creative force in the lives of
those in need. Though both sin gravely, the priest who fails to
work, with sweat and prayer, at his Sunday homilies is more
in violation of the vow of celibacy than one who fornicates.
If this statement shocks it is because we've lost, if ever we've
had, the true meaning of the celibate life.

What, Lord, has celibacy meant for me? I think of the
priests and religious of my young years. My earliest recol-
lections are of one priest who was the town drunk, another
whom all of us kids loved and admired because he made spin-
ning tops for us and boats in bottles, and another who got us
organized and shaped us into basketball, baseball, and foot-
ball teams. I remember with great love the sisters who taught
me from the first to the eighth grade, who were like so many
demanding mothers from nine to three each school day and
for whom my whole family — parents, sister, aunts, uncles,
cousins — had the greatest respect, and sometimes fear! There
were the fathers and brothers who taught me in high school
and college, and most vivid in memory is the lay celibate
who incarnated my guardian angel, became my mentor, and,
though dead these many years, guides and inspires me still.
There were the priests and religious I'd heard or read about:
some of them saints and sometimes rebels like their Lord and
Master, others degenerate, terrible wasters and abusers of life
and love. And there have been the fathers, brothers, sisters,
cloisterd nuns of my Order, some of whom I've known almost

as well as myself, have known their struggles, their successes, and their failures.

Just a few of these would have been enough to help raise me to you, but *cumulatively* they stand as powerful, living witness, sign and symbol, of your transcendence. Most of them seem to me to have been much a part of *this* world with little enough of the transcendent manifest in them. Except for my cloistered sisters I don't think of them primarily as people of deep prayer, though many of them probably were and are; rather I've witnessed them as teachers, preachers, cooks, launderers, artists, confessors, wounded healers of body and spirit, tenders of the poor and rich alike, lovers and sometimes haters of life, sinners and sometimes saints, believers in an afterlife with you as their supreme love, yet very much reluctant to leave this life no matter how painful it might be at times. Still it has been in and through them, their often prodded and prodding service, that I've come to know you as here within this world but more, as infinitely beyond it. More than your written word, much more, they have spoken and continue to speak to me of your infinite magnitude, and it's in and through them that I learned your written word. Even the radical failures among them. . . if only at one time in their life they were inspired to vow to move beyond the world in love, they've thus added to the witness to something within the human heart that longs for transcendence and thus have helped keep the rest of us from being smugly sure that everything is only here and now.

It's not so much individual celibates who have been a sign to me of your transcendence, but the living fact of celibacy itself. In the same way the living fact of marriage symbolizes for me your intimate presence more than individual married couples. Celibacy proclaims that the yearning for intimacy in body and spirit can only be fulfilled in you: "I am the promise of that which cannot be held," says the woman in your poet's play, "and my grace consists precisely in this."

But as with your miracles, without faith — that vision of the heart — neither marriage nor celibacy prove anything, except, perhaps, the futility of everything.

And my own celibacy? Whatever failures in love there have been I think that after all these years I'm still a loving person. I think of all I could have done and should be doing now for so many in need. All the world is crying out for help and here I sit at this machine trying to make sentences. Yet it's love within me, isn't it, Lord, that keeps me here in the hope that the words will do some good somewhere, that they *are* doing good here and now as by your grace they reach into some heart in need of them? I wish I might do more. Help me.

But for me my celibacy has meant primarily my relation to you as you are in yourself. All these years of being alone with you. Even when I've been with others it's been you alone I've been with. Like an introverted fanatic, I'm talking to you all the time, listening to you, listening *for* you. Even when I've sinned and tried to shut you out you've been there watching and waiting, and I'd know it all along. I'd hate you for it and love you for it. When I really think about it, as now, I find that it's true, you're the only one in my life. There are the others, the whole world in fact, but only within or beside you. I can be alone with you, but never alone with them. There it is, for my joy and my sorrow you are the only love of my life. It's a feeble, often reluctant love, I know, but it is love. If only it might grow from the mere spark that it is into the flame it's meant to be, you and I could be so happy together such that the whole world, and not just some small corner of it, might begin to take notice and recognize you as the great and loving God you are. Let it be!

We begin our lives not as lone, isolated individuals, but as family: it's within and through the communion of husband and wife that the child is conceived and born. Even those hundreds of thousands of years ago it seems likely that humankind began as family: "Male and female he created *them*." The earliest pictures we have of Christ is as family: in his mother's womb, lying in a manger surrounded by his parents, and brought back into family after having struck out on his own in Jerusalem. All a vestige, I should think, of the community which is God himself: Father, Son, and Mother Spirit. In the beginning was the family.

Yet today so much militates against marriage and family, such that more and more, at least in our western world, it's the individual, not the family, that's regarded as the basic unit of society. We care less and less for family rights as we become more and more entrapped in the rights of the independent, self-centered individual. So we have the "experimental marriage": Try it and see if you like it — as though such brief encounters were at all similar to the lifelong commitment of traditional marriage. There's the "temporary marriage," part of our throw-away society: Use each other up and then get yourselves other mates, whatever the consequences for you, your partner, and the children. There's sexual love without marriage, which leads to sex without love. There's marriage exclusive of children . . . the threat and fear of a population explosion . . . the economic difficulties of family life. And there's the pain of marriage and family: the joy, yes, but also the suffering of living close and becoming *one*, which means that when one is in pain or lost so also is the other.

But whatever the difficulties and pain of familial marriage, whatever the propaganda against it, people still long for it. It's a drive within, less obvious than that for food and drink, perhaps, but more deeply ingrained. Some may be afraid to bind themselves to the lifelong commitment that such marriage demands but this is only because they see how often it fails. Still, let the love of two people reach a certain depth and, whatever their fears, they're drawn into a marriage that they intend to be neither temporary nor experimental but till death, and beyond if possible. Even those whose marriages have failed with deep hurt on both sides find that as the wounds heal they begin once again to long for marriage and hope the next one will last.

That the child is of a piece with this longing is evidenced in striking ways. Several times in the college which was my "parish" for many years I've watched the young women's eyes light up when a baby was brought into their midst. Each would take the child in her arms and at that moment would appear as intimate with the child as though she were the mother. I've listened to the grief of married couples who were childless and frustrated in their attempts at adoption. Even more than their love for each other, it seems, was their love for the child that was not yet theirs, and perhaps never would be.

But the difficulties of marriage are real and sometimes insurmountable except for some extraordinary help. This is why marriage had to be raised to the level of a sacrament, had to be blessed, shot through with grace. And the sacrament isn't just the wedding ceremony when vows are made and blessed and prayers are offered for the happy and fruitful endurance of the love. It's this but so much more. It begins in these moments of mutual surrender and joy but it enters deep within the couple and is carried with them out of the church and into every second of the rest of their lives.

The sacrament is the graced instinct to be careful with love. We tend to take those we love for granted. We treat them as though we knew them. Yes, but also we should treat them as though we did not know them, which is nearer the truth. Someone has remarked that love is a fragile thing. You bet it is. This is why it lies broken all over the place. The sacrament is there to tell the married this and to help them reverence as well as love each other, help them to never take one another for granted, to give each other space, to listen to each other and help each other to grow.

It's the graced instinct to face and struggle through the inevitable pain of marriage and to see the worth of that pain. One of the sad characteristics of our time is the tendency to give up too soon. I don't say simply give up. Often there's not much else we can do. Pain can become intolerable; in a family, where several are involved, it is multiplied and intensified accordingly. Nice if we could all be strong enough to remain in communion with each other no matter what the cost. But frailty is our name. Your grace, Lord, is there, I know, to make us strong in our weakness, but it works in strange ways, and maybe the strength it gives doesn't come till far down the line after we've been crushed and defeated time after time.

I don't speak simply of giving up but of giving up "too soon," especially in the matter of love. Two people fall in love, marry, have children. They encounter trials along the way but their love carries them through. Then the love seems to diminish and maybe vanish altogether. The "fire," they say, is no longer there. At the same time the trials grow more severe, there are misunderstandings, recriminations, then silence, then separation and finally divorce and all the havoc it works, all within the space of a relatively few years. The *special* grace, the sacrament, of marriage is not so much to take away the pain but to keep us from running from one form of life and pain into another; to help the married see the worth of *their* pain as an instrument to bring them closer to each other, an invitation to look through and beyond it to the deeper love that lies on the other side.

And so the sacrament is an instinct to pray. In order to see the worth of pain and penetrate into deep love one must have the vision and the will for it. But this comes only when our very limited vision and will are stretched by those of God that become one with ours through prayer. The sacrament lodged within the married inspires prayer toward other ends also. Under its impulse, they pray to overcome the social obstacles to marriage and family. Here again it's a matter of vision and deep love in order that the narrowness and super-ficiality of a permissive society be surmounted. The married must continually lift up their minds and hearts to God, live in *his* world, so that they will not be overcome by the worst in this one.

They pray to see deeply into each other, for worshiping the divine in the beloved. How else love another with a love worthy of her except reach to God within her? What Jesus said is true of all, but especially of our special love: "In so far as you did this for one of the least of these brothers of mine, you did it to *me*" (Mt 25:40). Again, here is the need for penetrating vision which comes only through prayer.

They pray to see deeply into God. Most of us have super-ficial notions of and attitudes toward God. Few see him as he really is. The sacrament of marriage is given that husband and wife might find God visibly in each other and their children but also beyond themselves in the lightsome darkness of faith. Thus knowing a goal beyond themselves and this world they may be of help to each other in moving toward and reaching it.

Grounded in prayer, they may now be able to take the long view with regard to their children. Parents are constantly con-cerned about their children, and they should be. They worry over their physical and mental health, their education, their morals and faith. "What has happened to my children? What have I done wrong?" — legitimate laments over wayward chil-dren, perhaps, but quite possibly the product of myopia. Your children aren't just yours, not even mainly yours. They're God's, and God has purposes for them beyond your imag-inings and plans. He loves them and will care for them. So instead of *just* worrying and fretting why not pray to this great God beyond as well as within this world that he provide for them? If prayed well and unceasingly, that prayer of yours will, like St. Monica's for *her* child, succeed, perhaps not in your time and place, but in God's; and that's all that really matters.

In this crucial matter of marriage and family we have to be especially watchful of the world. We're told that marriage and family are going out of style. Well, what's coming in? Free love, with all its tragic, physical disease and spiritual degeneracy? The gay or contraceptive "marriage" in which introverted couples frustrate the social dynamism of love and so frustrate love altogether? No marriage or family at all with resulting loneliness in an already too lonely world? Familial marriage has its difficulties and a far from perfect history, but before writing it off, consider the alternatives; consider, too, if we've made proper *sacramental* use of it as outlined above.

So much can and should be done by all of us to preserve and promote family life. The married themselves should realize the power of the sacrament and continually draw upon its grace. The government should protect the family by making it economically and politically possible and inviting. Single people hoping for marriage should prepare for it as sacrament with all this entails and, in whatever their occupation, promote the common good by fighting the lies aimed against the family. And those vowed to celibacy, especially, must make it their highest priority to help the married realize the full potential of the sacrament.

One further brief word about marriage and family. We're continually reminded of the imminence of a population explosion and therefore of the dire need to limit and even nullify family. Soon, it's said, each of us will scarcely have one square foot of ground to stand on and not a morsel of food to eat.

I'm certainly no expert in demography, but I've often observed the earth as I've flown across these United States, Canada, Mexico. I've also studied maps of Russia, China, Africa. And I find little more than empty space! Uninhabitable, I'm told. So my ancestors were told that large areas of California were uninhabitable because they were dry and sterile desert. And now those very regions are what make California the fifth largest agricultural *nation* in the world! Why not apply some of the same creative imagination and expertise to other regions (though with less greed and greater care) and so make homes to live in and produce food enough to live by? Now, not just for a single state or nation but the whole of our world.

But whatever population explosion may be in the offing there's another that is more imminent and more serious, more imminent and serious too than the great nuclear explosion we dread, and that's the blow-up of the family. It will be the ground and cause of every other major tragedy of human origin, the beginning of a chain reaction that nullifies all. When its source and center fails the whole of the world comes tumbling down. So we'd better shore up the family or say goodbye to everything.

"Wait without love . . ." What do I mean, Lord, when I say I love you? I don't imagine or think of you then as a man, not even the man Jesus. I suppose because of my macho breeding it's difficult for me to say "I love you" to a man. Do I think of you then as a woman? I'd feel comfortable enough saying this to the right woman. But then I'd mean something much different than when I say it to you. I guess I just don't know what I mean, and yet I say the words to you over and over again and something in me makes me say them and my heart responds to them. I must mean something far beyond "love," as you are far beyond any other beloved. I guess I just have to wait until you give me to see what my words mean, what my heart is aiming at. All I know now is that you are someone much greater than any of those whom I love, and my "love" for you so totally different than any I have for them. *In coelo totaliter aliter*!

NINE

Intimations
of Immortality

Central in the teaching of Christianity is the resurrection of Christ and, in and through his resurrection, our own. Stripped of all theological complexity and nuance the doctrine means quite simply that death does not have the final say. As there is life before death, so is there life after death.

For the Christian this means *personal* immortality: I, Stan Parmisano, as Stan Parmisano (though vastly improved, I hope!) will survive my death. Thus it was with Jesus' resurrection, after which mine is to be patterned. Jesus insists that it is truly he himself, the one whom his disciples had known before and during his passion and death, who is appearing to them. "See by my hands and my feet that it is I myself. Touch me and see for yourselves; a ghost has no flesh and bones as you can see I have" (Lk 24:39). Jesus is quite different than what he had been — his disciples are incredulous, can't recognize him initially — and yet the same — they do recognize him once they take a second look: "It is the Lord . . . My Lord and my God" (Jn 21:7; 20:28). Christianity believes it's the same for all the saints. They have not been absorbed into some distant or abstract divinity, they have lost none of their "personality"; rather their persons have been intensified and expanded. A Francis, a Dominic, a Teresa, a Catherine are not less persons after death but more.

For the Christian it also means *immediate* survival. True, Jesus was some two or three days in the tomb before rising, but in Christian tradition he was alive all during this time: while his body rested in the tomb his spirit was "harrowing hell," liberating the just from their afterlife exile. Jesus himself seems to have suggested instantaneous survival when he toyed with Martha about dead Lazarus. Did she believe in the resurrection? Yes, "on the last day." Jesus' response is a startling corrective: "*I* am the resurrection and the life; he who believes in me, even if he die, shall live; and whoever lives and believes in me shall never die" (Jn 11:26). In other words, for those who believe in Jesus, immortality isn't somewhere down the line but at the very moment of death or what looks like death.

Such has been traditional Christian belief, but, as so much else of tradition, it has been challenged in our time, not just from outside the church but from within. There are those Christians, Catholics among them, who have no belief at all in immortality. "When it's over it's over," as a dear church-going eucharist-receiving relative of mine put it. A good nun of many years asked me in all seriousness: "Do you really think there's life after death?" These aren't rare exceptions. A new mentality has been formed, an altered social context that's challenged our belief in immortality as in so much else.

Working against belief in an afterlife is the all-pervasive materialism, scientific and otherwise, of our time. People might talk about spirit but they're immersed in matter, in that which is bound by time and space. Atoms come together by chance or law to form life but they just as mysteriously break apart unto death and corruption. Our concern is only for the visible, the tangible, that which gives pleasure and comfort to our bodies. As for "spirit" with its so-called delights, at most it can only be some tenuous form of matter dispersable at death as the rest of its kind . . .

> De Bailhache, Fresca, Mrs. Cammel, whirled
> Beyond the circuit of the shuddering Bear
> In fractured atoms . . .

There are those who claim that even should there be an afterlife it's no use talking about it since we don't know what we're talking about. It's as St. Paul said: "Eye has not seen, nor ear heard . . ." And when we do try to talk about it we degenerate into childish absurdities . . . as, quite unfairly but still significantly, recorded by Diane Keaton in her mischievous film *Heaven*.

There are still others who may believe in an afterlife but think that it's unworthy of real love to look to it. We should love God not for any reward that might come of it, some heaven that will compensate for all our suffering and service. Love God for love's sake. That should be compensation enough. Further, it distracts us from concern for this life and present justice. Marxist critique of Christianity is sympathetically quoted: Promise the poor pie in the sky and then you don't have to worry about giving them some of the pie here and now. If justice is sure to come in an afterlife then we don't have to labor for it in this one.

As for Christ's own resurrection a whole new way of reading the gospels makes it, according to some, problematic. Could it be simply a myth, a fantasy invented by the early church to encourage spiritual or moral regeneration? Our rising is not to be in some unknown future after death, but *now* as we become new persons according to the example of the heroic living and dying Christ.

But whatever the arguments and prejudices to the contrary, belief in personal immortality is difficult to kill — like God himself, who may seem dead in a given nation, culture, individual life but keeps rising from the dead, often stronger

and more vital than before his demise. Even scientific materialism, which was once thought to have dealt the fatal blow
to the belief, has for some years now spoken more modestly,
not because it's discovered "spirit" but because it has recognized the mystery of matter. In one of the sessions of a
parapsychology course I was teaching I had the chairman of
our physics department lecture the class on matter. He began:
"You think spirit is mysterious. Wait till you hear about matter!" And in reality are matter and spirit, body and soul, so di-
chotomized as they are in our minds? For present-day science
the question of personal immortality is far from being a closed
question.

Indeed, even in the heyday of scientific materialism — the
last of the nineteenth and the first half of the twentieth century — there were those practiced in science who thought the
question still open. What came to be known as parapsychology
had its birth in this very question. Reputable scientists such
as Joseph and Louisa Rhine, J. Gaither Pratt, and Gertrude
Schmeidler, investigated in the lab, in controlled experiment,
the possibilities of consciousness untrammeled by the materialistic categories of space and time, while equally respected
psychologists such as Frederic Myers and Edmund Gurney
dealt as scientifically as possible with on-the-spot "apparitions." Whatever one may think of their conclusions it must
be recognized that interest in the question of personal after-
death survival and an open mind to consider it occurred even
among the better scientists of the day.

One need not, then, think of oneself as scientifically naive
for believing in personal immortality or overly credulous because he or she respects experiences of others that seem to
come from "beyond." I myself have encountered in others,
whose intelligence and honesty I credit, experiences that suggest something more than only this life. Not the most remarkable of these but, for some reason, that which has made the
greatest impression on me was the experience of "Jean." She

was at the time a successful lawyer, and her husband an associate professor in one of our better secular universities. Neither of them seemed to have any interest in religion or belief in an afterlife. Jean's father, whom she loved very much, died. Some days after the funeral she lay in bed at night with her husband. She started to drift off but was suddenly awakened as she heard her name called. She asked her husband what he wanted, but he was sound asleep. She lay back again, awake and alert. Again she heard her name, and this time she knew it was her father. She doesn't know why but she replied: "Dad, what do you want us to do with the property?" The answer was audible, clear, and gentle: "Jean, Jean, if only you knew how little all this really matters." And that was it.

Jean had experienced nothing like this before and, to my knowledge, nothing like it since. The obvious explanation is that it was all a vivid dream; your reputable parapsychologist would immediately discount the experience as proof of nothing but grief and anxiety. But you can't tell Jean that. I don't know that the experience has altered her opinions about religion or the afterlife one jot, but she insists it was no dream. It was her father's voice in very reality.

I suppose Jean's experience appeals to me because it recalls, and yet is worlds apart from, my own experiences when my parents died. When my mother died I can't recall even dreaming of her let alone hearing her voice from the other side. Yet I was so grief-stricken that for more than a week I could scarcely breathe at night in bed. I would have to get up and pace the floor till I was exhausted and then chance sleep again. It was the opposite five years later when my father died. I could sleep all right, but every night for years after I would dream of him, quite vividly sometimes. Never, however, did I have actual sight or sound of him, though I longed for such. And never at any other time have I experienced apparitions, locutions, or any other manifestation of the afterlife. I think I've experienced something of God and what's to come but not in any tangible, visible, audible form; only in ways that are unspectacular, that might not seem of "experience" at all.

One of these ways is that of understanding, almost of rational argument. I have a number of "indications" of something more to come. Each by itself says little enough, but sometimes I *experience* them collectively and then they become for me what the poet has called "intimations of immortality": I could almost see, hear, touch, smell another life within and beyond this one.

There's Christ's word in the gospels: "Fear not, little flock, for it has pleased your heavenly Father to give you a kingdom . . . Come, you blessed of my Father, and possess the kingdom prepared for you . . . I am the resurrection and the life. He who believes in me, even though he die, shall live . . . In my Father's house there are many mansions; if it were not so I would have told you. I go to prepare a place for you . . . Amen, I say to you, this day you will be with me in paradise." Whatever some of the new exegesis and theology may say of these words, for me and for so many other simple and not so simple folk down through the ages they ring with literal truth. Jesus doesn't argue to an afterlife. He simply declares and points to it, and does it with impressive authority. I find myself listening and assenting with both mind and heart.

A second intimation for me is our mastery over matter and its limitations. We're said to be mortal because we're made up of that which upon death disintegrates, and because we're subject to matter's laws of time and space. But there's something within us that revolts against the very thought of death and continually pushes back death's domain. "Do not go gentle into that good night / Rage, rage against the dying of the light." And we refuse in often effective ways such limitations as space and time would impose.

The long history of medicine gives testimony to our struggle against corporal disintegration. And the history of the other sciences witnesses to our efforts to break out of the confinements of space and time. So, for instance, when we're housed on an area of land cut off from another by a body of water we build a boat, then a bridge, then a tunnel under the water. Still, this isn't enough. We want to escape the confines of earth altogether. So we construct an airplane and now we're up with the birds. Or we find that it takes too much time to walk from one place to another, and so we find a horse or camel to ride on, then we invent a train and an automobile to ride faster. Still we want to be even freer from spacial and temporal limitation, so we build faster and faster cars and planes, then spaceships . . . As though something deep within us were telling us that, though on first glance it may seem the contrary, our deepest nature is not to be of one time and a single space, but rather we are meant to be for always and everywhere.

Then there's the timelessness and spacelessness of human thought. Here I am in this little room shut off from the rest of the world. Yet with my thought I can reach outside to the garden, to the rest of the neighborhood, the city, the state, the country, the world; and I can reach up into the stars . . . I can think about the entire universe and God himself though I be confined in body to a room eight by twelve by twelve. With my mind I can as easily move from present to past, back through all of history to prehistory, to the absolute beginning of all where time and eternity merge. I can move into the future, in hope or in fear. I can project and plan and even make the future. Doesn't all this tell me that there is within me something spaceless and timeless that accordingly longs for its like? Something immortal that cries out for and demands immortality?

Human love in its fidelity is also a teasing intimation of immortality. Before the advent of materialistic and correspondingly cynical times, this used to be the stuff of a good deal of fine poetry.

> . . . Love is not love
> Which alters when it alteration finds . . .
>
> How do I love thee? Let me count the ways . . .
>   And if God choose,
> I shall but love thee better after death.

Whether or not love in fact is faithful is not entirely to the point here. What matters is that fidelity is conceived of as possible and it is desired. "I take thee to be my lawful wedded wife . . . until death do us part." And a truly loving couple want that love to endure even beyond death. This, perhaps, is one reason for the modification of the ancient marriage formula, eliminating all mention of death: "I promise to be true to you . . . *all the days of my life*." But in point of fact there *are* faithful, enduring loves with a desperate ache that what may be lost through death might be returned in a better life. So Robert Browning's response to his wife's words, quoted above, after she had died . . .

> Then a light, then thy breast,
> Oh thou soul of my soul!
> I shall clasp thee again,
> And with God be the rest!

That love in fact is faithful in some (many?) instances suggests that there is within *every* human being the capability of enduring fidelity, though often interfered with from one source or another.

But, you say, dogs and turtledoves are more universally faithful than men and women. Does this mean they are immortal too? Maybe. But there is a crucial difference in the loves. In the case of animals fidelity is instinctive: the turtledove *has* to love its mate, the dog must love the hand that feeds it. But in the human being love is free. It may be but need not be, in fact most often is not, enduringly faithful. There is a depth here — the profound depth of freedom — that's lacking in the animal. This freedom is an element unbound by physical nature and circumstance, something that rises above both, something truly and profoundly immortal.

Another intimation of immortality is sometimes recognizable in the aged. Body and spirit often seem to grow old together, and as the body disintegrates so does the spirit. But there are notable exceptions. I've known some who have seemed to grow younger in spirit as they've aged chronologically. They've kept the knowledge and memories of their past but have remained open to new ideas and ventures and have, indeed, helped create new ways of thinking and living. It's as though while their bodies were dying their minds and spirits were coming to new birth, with every indication that with the complete death of the body there would be a complete rebirth of spirit.

On the other hand I've also sadly experienced those whose minds seem to wither even before their bodies — memory, imagination, intelligence, zest for life all gone while the body is still young and strong. But even here there's reason to believe that spirit is still much alive within. We speak of loss of mind, loss of memory. But mind and memory are never lost, as evidenced in cases of amnesia cured and the mentally sick healed, and our unceasing efforts to work such cures. Mind and memory are always there, as alive as ever, only some obstacle, probably of body, interferes with their visible functioning, much as a defective radio won't pick up the sound waves that are nevertheless present to it. So with the spirit. Great spirited people may seem broken in spirit, but all their memories, all the good they have thought and done, evil suffered, grace given may well be within them still, and when their body dies their spirit is free to live again.

This intimation of immortality is even more startling in some children who seem to have a wisdom beyond their years. Once I was called to the hospital to baptize a boy of nine

years who was dying of Hodgkin's disease. When I arrived
the boy was unconscious, with his mother standing beside him.
She told me there was some mistake about the baptism, since
he had already been baptized. She said neither she nor her
husband were "believers" but for a long time her boy wanted
to be baptized, so finally they gave their consent and the local
parish priest did the job. I stayed on with her and the boy and
prayed in silence. Then the mother said: "His last words to me
were: 'I love you, mother. You worry too much about me.'"
And they *were* his last words. A nine-year-old boy. Where
did he get such wisdom and love, such magnitude of spirit?
Not turning inward and bemoaning his own fate but turning
outward in selfless love to his suffering mother. This wasn't
the result of chronology. Something within that child leapt
beyond the limitations of space and time . . . leapt, I should
think, all the way into heaven.

Finally there's the testimony of humankind, from the bur-
ial rites of prerecorded history to the beliefs, Christian and
otherwise, of the present. Except for a relatively few deviants
— most of our own "enlightened" era — all believe in some
form of afterlife, however crudely the belief may be expressed.
Evidently, something is there in the human spirit that doesn't
just rage against the dying of the light, but longs for the dawn-
ing of new light and life. All of this history added to my own
thought and experience, my conscious and unconscious belief makes for something of a vision. At times it's almost as
though I were already in this larger life beyond death. And as
I grow older I find myself becoming "curiouser and curiouser"
about it, and longing more and more to be a permanent part
of it.

As for those who deny or refuse to think or talk about an
afterlife, however sincere their thinking it has its limitations.
I may, for instance, not believe in an afterlife simply because

I never think about it: out of sight, out of mind, out of heart. Or I may not believe in it because I never do any thinking or living beyond my physical body or the body of this world. If all I'm concerned about is the comfort, pleasure, health of this corruptible and corrupting body of mine, if I never raise my mind to some transcendent beauty and truth then, yes, I form no idea of spirit, of that which is beyond body and all its limitations. All there is, then, is this life, and blessed little of it — when it's over it is indeed over.

Those who long and labor for justice for the poor here and now do right in insisting that our concentration should be on the betterment of this life, providing, of course, "betterment" involves the totality of life. But here precisely is where the afterlife and thought upon it has practical value. Jesus himself offered consideration of the afterlife not as a soporific and an escape from duty to the poor and needy but as a spur to it. "Come, you blessed of my Father . . . "

Jesus' parable of the sheep and the goats is not just a matter of reward or punishment in a hereafter. The afterlife is not discontinuous with this one but of a piece with it. As our life now enters into, is part of, the life to come, so is the latter an integral part of this life: It is this life in depth. To deprive the poor, or anyone, of belief in the life to come is to diminish their present life. If we and they would live and live fully in this life we must live in the belief that the fullness of life is yet to come and will be the fulfillment, the flowering, of this one.

We may think we are doing justice for the poor by focusing our and their attention only on this visible, tangible world of ours and laboring to make their present life happy. But no matter how hard we labor for justice it comes, if at all, slowly and only in bits and pieces, and most of the poor by far will continue to suffer and die through one form of injustice or another. Cruel, then, to deprive them of the consolation of the thought of justice hereafter while leaving them stripped of it now.

And is it so bad to look to the afterlife as reward for this one lived in love and service? Love should be its own reward, true, but it's the very nature of love to want to love forever. If all I wanted after death was the "reward" of some kind of palatial estate and the consolation of seeing my enemies "in another place," then certainly we should do without it, and we should wonder about the worth of a life that produced such a mentality and longing. But to want to continue to love and be loved by one's beloved is simply demonstration of the truth and depth of one's love.

Here is the final and most striking intimation of immortality for me — the love of God. If God loves me — and how else can I think of God except as loving me? — then he must love me *forever* . . . and me as I am and all that I might be. If we believe in God, the God of Jesus Christ, then there's no way out: There is life everlasting; and if we love God in return for his love of us, we must believe in, think about, be glad of this great reward he has stored up for us.

TEN

First and Last Things

"Out of my sight, you condemned, into that everlasting fire prepared for the devil and his angels!" (Mt 25:41, *NAB*).

"Not just purgatory but hell awaits those who could have done good and did not do it" (Oscar Romero, July 16, 1977).

Many think that Christianity invented hell — not Christ, who was tender, merciful, forgiving, but the church that grew up around and after him, and soon wandered from him. Not so. The conception antedates Christianity proper and is found among many peoples not christianized. It's one of the more persistent of archetypes. Sometimes "hell" designates simply the afterlife as a whole conceived as dark, lonely, a land of gloom and of mournful ghosts. Thus the *Hades* of the Greeks and Romans, *Taut* of the Egyptians, *Sheol* of the Hebrews, *Hel* of the ancient Germans and early Christians ("He descended into Hell . . ."), and all the various *under*worlds of other peoples, the world of the grave *under* the earth, a suffocating land of sad and oppressive silence.

But part of this underworld becomes specialized into a place of punishment, of real torment for evil done in one's lifetime. This locale takes over the name formerly designating the whole of the afterlife while new names are found for the happier regions: Elysium, Valhalla, Paradise, Heaven. The concept of hell as a "place" of punishment persists all through the medieval world, whether Christian or non-Christian, and has endured to our own day.

In recent times, however, belief in hell has all but vanished. Today not many, even among Christians, take hell seriously. It's thought of as a fading vestige of a primitive mentality darkened by violent and prurient interests, a belief, moreover, incompatible with the Christian God of absolute mercy and forgiveness. Yet see how slippery the archetype is: Do away with an invisible hell hereafter and it turns up in quite tangible forms here and now, in society at large and in one's personal life. We think of the hell erupting in Hitler's Germany and Stalin's Russia, in current wars and terrorism, in the drug scourge, in the physical abuse and mental crippling of children. We think of the film and literature of our day, at once reflective and creative of all the violence, despair, emptiness, boredom of the traditional hell. Dante's hell was love gone awry. For the contemporary poet it's pretty much the same, only the hell is limited to here and now, though some would seem to leave the possibilities open:

> Great lovers lie in hell, the stubborn ones
> Infatuate of the flesh upon the bones;
> Stuprate, they rend each other when they kiss;
> The pieces kiss again — no end to this.

The conception of hell doesn't originate in human morbidity, though some of its coloring does. There is a manichaean strain in most of us that luxuriates in evil and builds it, at least in imagination, into worlds of horror and torment. We tend to exaggerate evil where it is and create it where it is not: so a literature of ghosts and monsters, torture and murder, and a sad history of witch-hunting and persecution. Easy to see how out of such a mentality hell with all its trimmings might arise and endure.

But there are deeper, more likely origins. Karma, for one, the sense that however unjust the world may seem and be, at its heart is justice, which eventually is fulfilled, if not in this life then in another. This seems to be the *theological* reason behind the conception as it appears in some of the great world religions. All evil must be compensated for, balance must be restored, justice fulfilled before final rest, peace, joy, nirvanah is reached. Hell is for those whose hearts are set against this universal law; purgatory or reincarnation for those anxious to satisfy it. Here at work is the law behind Jesus' obvious preference for the poor: "My son, remember that during your life you had your fill of good things, just as Lazarus his fill of bad. Now he is being comforted here while you are in agony" (Lk 16:25).

But Christianity teaches that there are still deeper roots to hell. They're lodged in the great gift of human freedom. Kierkegaard speaks of the event of God's having created vis-a-vis himself a being who is free as the cross upon which philosophy was crucified. Yes, the great mystery. But few face up to it and realize its implications. If I am free then ultimately it is within my power to accept or reject the very Giver of the gift, and God is bound, by his own truth, to respect my choice.

Thus, it is not God who creates or condemns to hell, but the free human being who makes and perseveres in a radically wrong choice or, which is the same thing, has failed to make the right one. Instances abound of men and women making a hell of this life, for themselves and others. The drug, alcohol, or sex addict, the envious and the jealous, those consumed by anger and hate, rapists and murderers, all are in a hell of their own making and they draw countless others into their torment. We think of an Hiroshima and a Nagasaki, an Auschwitz and a Dachau, that not God but a misguided human freedom has turned into monstrous infernos. We now know that if the end of the world should come it will not be the work of a vengeful

God but of a gifted freedom that has lost its center and pushed the fateful and fatal button.

If we are the ones who make hell now, why not hereafter? If we do little if anything to love God and banish hell in this life why should we suppose things will be different in the next? Might not those in the hell of the afterlife strangely continue on in it rather than humbly submit to love and its demands, just as many who know they're even now in hell turn their backs on love, and Love itself, having become frightfully enamored of their torment? "I'll be damned if I'll apologize," says the man in C.S. Lewis' parable of hell. The terrible thing is, there are people who do say and mean this, before they die, as they die, and . . .

How conceive of hell? Better not try. People have tried in the past and only succeeded in making the whole thing ridiculous, scary ridiculous but nonsense all the same. Hell is the epitomy of evil and evil borders on nothingness. In terms of the old theology, which still has a lot going for it, evil is privation, that is, nothing where something should be. I should be loving; the evil, then, lies in my *not* loving. But how describe or depict "nothing"?

Yet the images Christ himself gives of hell are salutary as all that Christ has given us. He speaks of it as fire. We think, then, of hell's painful nature, but more as a destructive force, and still more as that which diminishes. Toss a piece of paper in the flames and see how it curls over on itself and becomes smaller and smaller till all that remains is a pinpoint of ash. So the hell of hell, now and hereafter: We close in on ourselves and become less and less till we are reduced to almost (almost!) nothing. And so the host at the gospel banquet says to the foolish virgins who demand entrance: "I know you not." Why? Because there's nothing to know.

Christ speaks of the son of man cursing the evil ones on the last day: "Depart from me..." Rejection. In our time we understand the pain embodied in this word and know the horror, the hell, of its consequences: rejected children and the scars dug into them because of rejection and the hell they themselves create in the future because of it; the old who are cast off; men and women fired from their jobs; the social outcast, Yankee go home; Dogs and Niggers not allowed; *Keep Out* coldly written over one we want to give our love to. Terrible experiences in and of themselves, but also as images of something just as bad or worse to come.

In his parable of Dives and Lazarus, Jesus has Abraham say to Dives in hell: "Between us and you a great gulf has been fixed, to prevent those who want to cross from our side to yours or from your side to ours" (Lk 16:26). Absolute separation from everything beautiful and worthwhile, separation not just from God but from everything that stands in his light — friends, music, warm human love, the sun and stars... Now when we reject God much of him is still available to us: His light filters through to us from many different sources. But in the dark of hell there is always and only our self with nothing "out there" to give us comfort.

Yes, the dark of hell. So Jesus' other image: "As for this good-for-nothing servant, throw him into the darkness outside where there will be weeping and grinding of teeth" (Mt 25:30). Once I visited Alcatraz Island and was shown the cell of solitary confinement. Small, with two steel doors at its entrance. The guide asked me if I'd like to try it out. Sure. I went in and heard the heavy door ring shut. Everything went black. Then I heard the second door slam. Now the blackness turned to syrup. I could feel the weight of it upon me and I could scarcely move nor did I want to. I could understand how one so confined for any length of time would make his way to one of the cell's crabbed corners, sink into it, and under the weight of that terrible night become and remain fetal. Yes, in hell there is only one's self and whatever else there may be serves only to turn one inward to deeper, heavier, more stifling dark, like the last stages of severe and chronic depression.

These are not my images, they don't arise from any morbidity of mine. Jesus is to blame. Evidently he wanted to impress upon us the seriousness of our life and death and of our right use of our greatest gift. I myself don't know that I take Christ altogether seriously in the matter of hell. Once I feared it, and an eternity of it, and I became morbidly obsessed with the thought of it. For some months with pen in hand I tried to argue myself out of it. After much agonizing I finally reached the more or less satisfying conclusion that though hell was quite possible for me God's great mercy would in fact keep me from it, providing I at least *tried* to love and serve him. After all these years it has become even less a threat to me. I don't know whether this is because of a deeper faith in God's great mercy (I'm saved!?) or less appreciation of freedom and the exigencies of justice. If the former I'm grateful, if the latter I trust and pray proper light will be forced upon me in due time.

"In my father's house there are many mansions" (Jn 14:2, *NAB*).

If our gift of freedom, through misuse of it, enables us to descend so low as hell, we can also, through our free acceptance of God's great grace, rise as high as heaven. Such is the teaching of Christianity, and such, as far as I can measure it, is my personal belief. Heaven, like hell, is not an exclusively Christian conception. Paradise, Elysium, Valhalla, Nirvanah, a Happy Hunting Ground, Green Pastures . . . always a looking forward, or a looking back, on some ideal place or state of undiluted happiness. Something in our nature keeps telling us we're meant for something more . . . something once had, maybe, and lost, but to be had again if worked at.

As with hell, we have to take great care when we attempt to conceive heaven. In fact, we ought to begin, as does St. Paul, with the realization that, like its opposite, it's inconceivable. Heaven, in Christian tradition, is God himself, and who can describe the living God? But once we accept it as mystery then we may begin modestly to say something about it in order to keep mindful of its reality here and hereafter. The preacher's paradox: Words say almost nothing about God, but unless we use them, with care, we lose both God and heaven!

I find in Christ once again a hint as to how to think about heaven. "Anyone who does not welcome the kingdom of heaven like a little child will never enter it" (Mk 10:15). Why not, then, try to get into the mind of a child and see what we come up with? I don't mean a child's mind as it may all too soon have been spoiled and scarred by a sad, cynical world, but as it is in its innocence. If such innocence were presented properly with the traditional elements of heaven how would it respond? Such inquiry may help resurrect the child long since buried in ourselves, and we may then begin to glimpse something of what heaven is like.

Heaven is where the angels are. Children are adept at projecting a world other than this one and live within it as though it alone was real. For them fiction or fantasy *is* reality. We think of Alice's Wonderland, Dorothy's Oz, every boy's Treasure Island, all of a fairly recent past and still enthralling children today. But we also are much aware of updated versions of the same, like the worlds of *Star Trek*, *Star Wars*, and all the imaginative and explosive films of a George Lukas and Steven Spielberg. Even adults are drawn into such fantasies, because of their beauty, certainly, and that paradisal archetype within all of us, but also because of a common belief that there are *in fact* other worlds inhabited by living, intelligent creatures, and of a type and species higher than our own.

Is it so difficult, then, to concede the possibility, even the likelihood, of a real heaven, peopled by creatures alive

like ourselves but vastly different and superior? We're like
fishes deep down in the sea, *our* world. We have no idea
of what's above, if anything. Now and again we may come
close enough to the surface to note something other than the
dark we're inured to — a thinning out of the dark in what we
come to call light — and we may begin to speculate (we're
intelligent fish!) about what's beyond. But suppose we should
get close enough to the surface to leap out of our ocean. Now
we see for the first time sky, sun, stars, and feel something
upon our scales other than water. Suppose, just suppose we
should then leap up onto dry land and suddenly acquire legs
and the capacity to breathe air. Now we walk on land, we see
trees, insects, animals, all so different from ourselves and each
other or anything we've ever dreamed of. Then we wobble into
some city and behold bridges, cars, skyscrapers, and human
beings . . . All these other *worlds*!

Such may well be this "land" of joy after death. Not just
extraterrestrial life, but quite literally life out of this *world*;
not populated with bodily creatures resembling ourselves but
creatures of an entirely different dimension. "What no eye
has seen and no ear has heard, what the mind of man cannot
visualize; all that God has prepared for those who love him" (1
Cor 2:9). Our eyes, ears, minds may not be able to make such
a leap, but our hearts can, and sometimes do take a modest
step or two in its direction.

Heaven is where those we've loved are or will be, and we,
by God's good grace, will be with them again. So St. Thomas
argues that love bonds formed now will endure in heaven,
for the simple reason that heaven is the *fulfillment* of all that
is best in this life. We tell, or used to tell, our children that
grandma and grandpa, or maybe mom or dad, were in heaven,
and they could believe this and take some consolation from
it: What's lost would one day be returned. Here again some
of the best of fiction finds its center: A Tristan and Isolde, a
Romeo and Juliet, a Cathy and a Heathcliff . . . lovers' longing

for lasting union and consummation beyond the grave is all but universal, however awry it sometimes may go and however thwarted it may become through a faithless denial. Nostalgia for heaven, precisely as the home of friends we think of as already there . . . mere fantasy? Not if the heart is listened to as well as the mind, the child within as well as the adult.

But what of those whom I've loved who might happen to end up in hell while I'm in heaven? How could I possibly be happy if such were the case? The answer is stark but soberingly clear. If they have truly loved me then they are in heaven or close to it: just a bit of real love is too much for hell. If their love was false then, like God, I shall not know them, and therefore not miss them, for nothing will be there to know or miss.

Heaven is where we'll always be happy. Adults can't imagine or really accept this. The older we become the more happiness seems to recede till most of our life is pain and loneliness and times of happiness are brief intervals in between. But with children it's the other way around. Even abused, so-called "unhappy" children still have the hope of happiness. Part of their pain is their confusion: Life should be happy but for some strange reason it's not. Adults, on the other hand, though they might possibly accept heaven as a place of peace, of "eternal rest," surcease of pain, balm of hurt minds, baulk at endless happiness. Belief in and desire for it usually passes with the passing of childhood.

But the child is still within us, though it be buried under layers of misery, and it can and should and must be resurrected. "Unless you become as little children . . ." I, as most people by far whom I've known, have had times of happiness. I don't mean times of contentment over a good meal, a new car, a kind and flattering remark, or even times of grand success in some important endeavor. I mean moments of deep happiness, almost of vision . . . like falling in love, the kind of love that alters the whole of your life; like reaching the summit of a mountain and finding the world open up and out into infinity; like scrubbing tables in the early morning and feeling lonely and abandoned and then catching heaven in a thread of sunlight across your hand; like "music heard so deeply/ That it is not heard at all but you are the music / While the music lasts"; like falling deep into prayer and only afterwards realizing you'd almost *seen* the Lord. The trouble is, we forget. The poet speaks of "the years of love that have been forgot / In the hatred of a minute." The remembrance of all that happiness gone because of all the pain. But happiness was there, a foretaste of the heaven we were made for. We can and should remember it. Then heaven once again might become real to us.

Heaven is where God is. Children can accept this without a lot of doubt and qualification. They might think of Father God, Mother Mary, Brother Jesus . . . like their own family if that family is right, or like their family should be if it's not. But adults can and should see more deeply into the proposition. Many find boring the thought of heaven as the vision of God — the so-called "beatific vision." Just looking at God forever doesn't on the surface appear very attractive. But God isn't something or someone out in space to be gazed at from afar or even up close. God is a whole infinite world unto himself, outside us and within us, with depth upon depth upon depth of truth and beauty. *If* we should tire of "looking at" one facet of God and turn away, we find that we're now gazing upon some other even more attractive nuance of God's beauty . . . something like listening to Beethoven's *Ninth* or Handel's *Messiah*: always something new and fresh and startlingly beautiful.

We're not to think of heaven as a state of just looking at God, but rather looking *with* him at whatever else may be. Think of being at the ocean with someone you love and together watching a glorious sun rise up or go down. It's so much more beautiful because of the one you're with. As here in this life, but much more so in heaven, God is the background, the atmosphere of all we see and hear, as well as the one with and within us doing the seeing and hearing. Not much, I should think, that's boring in this.

Heaven is where we're always awake, alive, and never grow weary. In the time of Advent the church sings out: "See the Lord is coming and with him all his saints. Then there will be endless day." Children would respond most favorably to this aspect of heaven. To be always awake, never having to go to bed except when utterly and irretrievably exhausted, such is the way of the child . . . and also of those who are deeply engaged in life or in some great love of their life. The rest of us, being jaded and bored, no longer curious about or interested in life, rather long for the night and that "eternal rest" that closes all. But again, we are to become as little children, that is, to wake up and begin to "see" once more. So much in life, outside and within us, and so little we're aware of. In Thorton Wilder's *Our Town* little Emily dies and on the other side of things she's lonely for her family and wants to return. She's warned that she won't like it, but she wants to go back anyway. So she's given a trial run. Back in spirit in her home she's happy at first but then begins to feel bad and soon discovers why: Her mother and father and brother are doing their own little things and hardly notice each other. She cries out in spirit: "Stop and look at one another!" But they don't, perhaps because they can't. It's the living who are dead. Only in heaven do we at last come alive.

But heaven, as hell, is not just hereafter. It's meant to begin here and now, and only those who try to make heaven of this life, for others as well as themselves, will enjoy it in the next.

"I believe no happiness can be found worthy to be compared with that of a soul in purgatory except that of the saints in paradise; and day by day this happiness grows as God flows into these souls, more and more as the hindrance to his entrance is consumed" (St. Catherine of Genoa).

So much talk today in the west about reincarnation and so little about purgatory; yet basically their roots are the same: karma, and the belief that only when entirely purified of all dross will we be able to be one with the divine. I suppose one reason why reincarnation is in and purgatory out is because of the fascination with a religion or philosophy that comes from afar and boredom with one that's up close. Another is due to a superficial knowledge of both. In the east, which is its home, reincarnation is toward the future: purification that one might eventually be freed of the cycle of death and rebirth and be absorbed in the divine One. But western devotees often see it as a kind of game for social discourse that looks simply to the past — Who was I in a previous life? — with no relevance to future conduct and life. As for purgatory, Protestants have long since discarded it and Catholics no longer know what to make of it. Once a year in November and at funerals prayers may be offered for the dead. But is this an archaism, soon to go the way of fish on Fridays? Or is there still something to it, with present mind lagging behind past (and present) heart?

My preference is for purgatory, and for two worthy reasons. The first is my belief in the dignity and inviolability of each and every person. I am not Napoleon reincarnated nor was he Julius Caesar or Alexander the Great. Each of us is who we are and as such we are loved by God. Individual me, Stan Parmisano, *as* Stan Parmisano, is loved by God. I have *my* life to live, not someone else's; judgment, here and hereafter, is to be upon that. Hereafter there is not to be just Napoleon having come to perfection in me or someone else in the future, but Napoleon *and* me and billions of others. Heaven is to be a populous place, though not crowded since its "space" is the infinite reaches of God.

My second reason for preferring purgatory is that it is more finely imaginative. Reincarnation fits the materialistic mind and temperament. It is earthbound, the very thing it doesn't want but can't escape from. Like the whole conversation today about extraterrestrial life: Whatever *other* life there is must be linked to some material planet or star and must wear familiar antennae and space suits and travel in mechanical space ships, however sophisticated it all may be. But purgatory is of an entirely different dimension, as are heaven and hell. We may try to imagine it but once the image is formed we must let it go and be left simply with some afterimage or feeling, some guess or suspicion. Something of this world abides but the center is far from it. The movement is centrifugal not centripetal: inward, certainly, but an inwardness that opens out into regions far from those we now inhabit.

And so the sermon goes, at my favorite time of year . . .

During this month of All Saints and All Souls the church would have us turn our thoughts to what comes after death, particularly to heaven and purgatory. A rather difficult task that it asks of us, so little can we know of the afterlife. But as an old philosopher once told his students: Just a little knowledge about such things is worth more than a great deal of knowledge about lesser matters. For a few moments, then, come into my mind while I try to guess at something of the nature of purgatory.

In purgatory, the work of self-realization is completed in us: full knowledge and full mastery of one's self relative to God. It's not a time of trial, wherein we are to shape our choice either for or against God. That choice has already been made in *this* life and by God's special grace it is immersed now, and so shares, in the eternal, constant will of God. Freedom is still there, but, paradoxically, it's "limited" to moving and growing within that alone which makes it infinite and eternal.

It's like lovers here and now. Ask them if they're free to love each other and they'll say yes: Indeed they'll tell you they never knew true freedom until they found each other's love. Ask if they're free not to love each other and chances are the answer will be a definite no, for that would mean, among other tragedies, a loss of their freedom. So one in purgatory in the strength of some profound experience of God has the joyous security of knowing that she can never turn her back upon him. She is and must remain God's lover as also his beloved for eternity.

Purgatory is rather for the purification and perfecting of our love for God. For many this work is begun in this life; but in relatively few, I think, is it ever completed in this life. Most of us by the time death rolls round have a very imperfect knowledge of ourselves, and consequently we remain stunted in growth and limited in love. True, now and again we're drawn into the deep, we experience some vision of what we are, and are not, but this is fleeting. It's not long before we're up on the surface again, remembering little if anything of what we've seen. By death, then, we're only a fraction of what we might have been and could be, and we don't even know (though we guess at) our failure.

See what there is to know in us and master. There is, first of all, our soul or spirit — a tremendous reality embracing rather than embraced by our body — with its enormous faculties of intellect and will, memory and imagination. There's in us God's grace — his own ineffable life — particularly of faith, hope, and love, meant to invade and permeate our soul (and body) in its every level till we are completely beautiful with the beauty of God, perfectly disposed for the one added grace that will give us the very vision of God.

Such in sum, in ridiculous generality, is the good in us, and such is what is *meant* to be. But there's also evil in us, pockets of emptiness focused on things other than God: beliefs, hopes, loves other than the faith, hope, love given by

God toward God — all of which tends to overgrow the good
and swallow it up. It checks and stifles what's meant to be
and leaves us betwixt and between. What do we really know
about any of this?

I know little of human nature in general. I know even
less of myself as an individual. What are my particular gifts,
and how much of what is meant to be *in me* is actualized?
What is my deepest motivation, my underground dynamic?
Has God's grace so infiltrated my soul that there is in it no
belief except that which is enveloped and directed beyond
itself by my Christian faith, no hope except for God and the
things that will get me God, no love but for God and for the
sake of God? "All is grace," said St. Thérèse in the days of
her last agony, *her* final purification. How much am *I* aware
of this and how much of my life is governed by it?

Once there was a young man who had lots of money. He
asked our Lord: "What must I do to gain eternal life?" Our
Lord answered: "Keep the commandments." The young man
replied: "But these I have kept from my youth." Then our Lord
looked on him with love and said: "If you would be perfect,
go, sell all you have . . . and come follow me." You know the
rest. The young man refused the offer. He turned and, says
the gospel, went away sad. Why "sad"? Because for the first
time in his life he realized fully that he did not altogether love
God. Face to face with Christ and Christ's truth he discovered
at last his true self and all that was wanting in him. He was
good, for he had always kept the commandments — no mean
feat! — and he came to Christ with the best of motives. But
evidently he was not good enough, and in that moment of
truth he realized it.

I am a good man, though certainly not rich and no longer
young. I am a practicing Christian: I believe (I believe), I hope
(I hope), I love (I think I love); I keep the commandments —
not from my youth, but now I do (more or less). But if Christ
should ask me to give *all* I have and *really* follow him —

sad, I should discover in myself many bonds that were not tied by God.

Even now, before the grand revelation, I sometimes hear faint whisperings as to the imperfect state of things deep down: those gnawing doubts and fears that keep eating away at my Christian creed — not quite compatible with a *perfect* faith; outcroppings of despair and sadness — where's my *perfect* hope?; and my loves — why do I say "loves" instead of "love," except my love be imperfect, and why don't I run to embrace Christ rather than merely passively suffer him to embrace me? And all those grand ideas I have of myself and all my touchy feelings — where's my faultless humility? And my petty anger and limping lust and . . . ? These rumors I hear, now and again. But what I most fear — and yet long for — is that moment of death when Christ will visibly look on me with love and ask me to leave *all*, for then I shall realize fully what I am, and am not.

What I most fear is purgatory. For this is purgatory: leaving absolutely all, except your own soul and the thought of Christ, who is God's love. Community will be there and the remembrance of a concerned community here — we are a communion of saints, here and hereafter — but it will expand rather than diminish the contemplation of your deepest self and the thought of your God, and will challenge you in some way to relive your failures and make them right. There'll be no radios or TVs to switch on, no cigarettes to reach for, none of the pleasures of poetry and music, no companions to joke with, no love or hate to distract you, no mystery stories, philosophy or theology books, no eating, no sleep, no joy and no pain that might for one moment draw you (as now it often does) from your task of self-realization in the still hidden presence of God. All you might have been and done, all you were and failed to acknowledge and be grateful for will more and more appear till it's all there before you, lived through again, and made perfect at last. And as you become more and more what you were meant to be the thought of God's love in you and for you will become clearer and more intense, till it gives way to vision — where before you had seen only yourself, now you see God.

Yes, I am a good man, and, please God, if I persevere in my goodness to death I shall win heaven — but, I suspect, not right away. God's great mercy wants for me the glory of truly winning heaven, not merely the grateful heart in accepting the gift. I'll have miles to go along the solitary and narrow way between death and heaven. God give me courage to go some of that way now.

"The bruised reed he will not crush; the smoldering wick he will not quench until judgment is made victorious. In his name the Gentiles will find hope" (Mt 12:20–21; Is 42:3–4).

I had a dream the other night. For several days and nights I had been restless. By day I was frustrated in my work, my temper was up, my prayer was fitful and anxious, I worried over church and world and over one person in particular. At night I'd toss and turn. I'd switch on the light, try to read, watch some late (or early) TV. I'd turn out the light again, thumb through my rosary. I even tried counting sheep, which would end up as lions and tigers, mad dogs and monsters. Then by a kind of miracle, it seems, I slept. It was a deep sleep through eight full hours. I awoke from it light and refreshed, and simply lay there savoring its aftertaste with no recollection of its substance. Then, more like a vision now than a dream, it all came back to me, scene by scene.

In panic I was running over moors I had once been on in England years ago. It was dark and drizzling and I was being chased by someone, something. Then, exhausted, my feet lumps of lead, I stopped and turned. The rain had ceased, and it was a clear, crystal day, and a little dog, bright-eyed and fawning, waited some three or four yards away. She looked up at me and said: "Why are you running? It's only me." I reached down to lift her to me, but she scampered away down a steep path all bordered with purple heather. She was laughing, and I laughed too as I ran after her.

Without my being aware of it, or caring apparently, the heathered path had turned to pavement and I was idly walking down my favorite street in San Francisco. It was a cold, crisp night. Cars on the sidewalk, people in the street, everyone bundled in their warm winter clothing. It was Christmas eve and it seemed the whole world was out enjoying it, for every race and every nation and every tribe from whatever country was there. With the others I was having a great old time, jostling and being jostled, admiring the trees and cribs and Santas and heaped-up packages in bright store windows. I heard myself saying over and over again: "This is the happiest. . . This is the happiest. . . This is the happiest Christmas I've ever had."

Then I saw her. She was standing alone in the narrow doorway of one of the more modest shops. She wore a Russian fur hat and a long fur coat, with one arm snugly cuddled in the sleeve of the other. I found her looking at me with large, smiling eyes, and I thought I recognized her. I walked up to her and said: "Didn't we meet somewhere — was it Rome, or possibly Paris?" She answered in the purest, most natural voice I'd ever heard: "I'm the one who brought you here. Are you enjoying the feast? I am. All my children from so far and so near. Like you they all thought they were lost, and they were. But they were lost only to be found and brought here to enjoy the Birth." I could say nothing as she spoke, or afterward. I could only listen and listen deeply, and I was still listening as she vanished from me and the dream dissolved.